The flowering of
Byron's Genius

The Flowering of Byron's Genius

Studies in Byron's
DON JUAN

By

PAUL GRAHAM TRUEBLOOD

"For I will teach, if possible,
the stones to rise against
earth's tyrants."
—BYRON

New York

RUSSELL & RUSSELL

To
Father and Mother

Preface

Lord Byron, relentless enemy of oppression and resolute champion of human freedom, was a leader in the vast social revolution of his era. In his great epic-satire, *Don Juan,* he gave powerful utterance to his "plain, sworn, downright detestation of every despotism in every nation." Today, when oppression is again rampant, Byron's satire possesses an immediacy and a pertinence so amazing as to create the impression of contemporaneousness.

The positive import of this masterpiece of social criticism has never received adequate recognition. This was first pointed out to me by Professor Newman Ivey White of Duke University, who at the same time encouraged me to undertake a series of studies which might constitute an introduction to a critical edition of *Don Juan.* In accordance with Professor White's suggestion, and with the benefit of his guidance, I pursued this series of studies, three of which comprise this present work.

In the first of these three studies I have made a detailed comparison of the early cantos of *Don Juan* with the later cantos, a comparison which reveals the distinct evolution of the poem from sportive satire to serious social criticism. I have concluded this study with an inquiry into the factors which may have contributed to this growth. In this connection I have noted particularly the influence, ordinarily ignored or minimized, of Teresa Guiccioli, as well as the very probable indebtedness of Byron to Henry Fielding. I am persuaded that the growth which *Don Juan* evinces is owing primarily to the inevitable flowering of Byron's satiric genius.

In my study of the contemporary reception of *Don Juan* I have confined my investigation to the English periodical reviews, the pamphleteer criticism having been definitively treated by Samuel C. Chew in his *Byron in England: His Fame and After-Fame* (London, 1924). My purpose has been to present the reviews of *Don Juan* which appeared in the English periodicals from August 1819 to April 1824 (the period during which the poem was published in groups of cantos), in order to appraise the criticism in the light of the prevailing critical prejudices of the day, and to determine the effect of the reviews upon Byron. My survey of the periodical criticism of *Don Juan* includes seventeen reviews not listed by Ernest Hartley Coleridge in his critical edition of *The Works of Lord Byron: Poetry* (London, 1898–1904). All these reviews are to be found in the notable collection of nineteenth-century periodicals maintained in the Library of Duke University. In my appraisal of the reviews of *Don Juan* I have been spurred by the words of Oliver Elton, who in his *Survey of English Literature, 1780–1830* has well said that "there has never been a sufficient reaction against the false censure of Byron." And I have been inspired by the distinguished example of my friend and professor, Newman Ivey White, in his analysis of the contemporary reception of Shelley in *The Unextinguished Hearth* (Duke University Press, 1938) and in his definitive biography of *Shelley* (Knopf, 1940).

The concluding study represents an attempt to establish the positive import of Byron's serious criticism of life in *Don Juan*. The general satiric character of the poem is a matter of common knowledge. Byron's debt to other satirists and the relation of his satire in *Don Juan* to his other satirical works has been adequately set forth by Hugh Walker in *English Satire and Satirists* (New York, 1925) and by Claude M. Fuess in *Lord Byron as a Satirist in Verse* (New York, 1912). Fuess also examines Byron's satiric method and manner; but he maintains that the poet's "broader philosophic satire . . . . is essentially shallow and cynical." Byron, he asserts, "took no positive attitude toward any of the great problems of existence." I have found, on the contrary, that a detailed and analytical examination of the objects of Byron's satire in *Don Juan* reveals the essentially constructive significance and effect of Byron's major satirical production.

My greatest personal debt, as I have already intimated, I owe to Professor Newman Ivey White for suggesting this undertaking, for unfailing encouragement and generous assistance, and for the inspiration of his example in creative scholarship. I am grateful to the Duke University Library for the opportunity afforded the student of English Romanticism by its distinguished collection of Byron and Byroniana as well as its rich store of literary source materials of the nineteenth century. In conclusion, I must express my deep appreciation to the Board and Directors of Pendle Hill for the year of study in Philadelphia which a Pendle Hill Scholarship made possible.

PAUL GRAHAM TRUEBLOOD

STOCKTON, CALIFORNIA
February 9, 1945

Contents

Chapter One

THE GROWTH OF
DON JUAN

I

THE MOOD OF THE EARLY CANTOS

Lord Byron was primarily a satirist. His poetical career began and ended with satire. The major poetic production of his early period was the neoclassic satire, *English Bards and Scotch Reviewers*. His last and greatest poetic production was his epic-satire of society, *Don Juan*. Following the trend of popular taste, Byron turned away, during his middle period, from satire to sentiment; *Childe Harold* was the result. But Byron did not renounce satire. William J. Calvert has justly questioned whether Byron ever truly identified himself with the romantic revolt.[1] Be that as it may, Byron's turning aside was only temporary. He could not long be satisfied with sentiment. His strongly satiric nature came to the fore again, and, permanently abandoning the Childe Harold role, Byron eventually found complete expression in seriocomic satire.

Byron's mind remained fettered until he found the poetic medium best suited to his genius. In *Don Juan* are perfectly blended for the first time in Byron's poetry the several elements of the seriocomic strain—the cool sarcasm, the serious reflection, the bizarre wit—which had appeared singly or in unfused combination in some of his

[1] William J. Calvert, *Byron: Romantic Paradox* (University of North Carolina Press, 1935), p. 61.

earlier poetry. This sportive mood, first manifested in certain of Byron's earlier verse, such as "Lines Written to Mr. Hodgson" (1809) and "The Devil's Drive" (1814),[2] emerged now and again in Byron's poetry, correspondence, and journals; but it did not reach full fruition until Byron had tried his hand at *Beppo* and had penned the first five cantos of *Don Juan*.

Venice, with its sunny skies, licentiousness, and gaiety, allowed Byron his full personal and mental freedom and, consequently, his artistic freedom as well. Smarting under the ostracism of English society and virtual exile in Italy, and determined to affect indifference to English censure, Byron, for a time, abandoned himself to a career of license, but without allowing this life to absorb him heart and soul. For he saw the comic aspect of his situation. Having put away the sad-hearted anguish, part fact and part affectation, of his youth, he began to see life with a clearer vision; emancipated from his former melancholy and mannerism he began to regard himself less seriously and his foes with ironical amusement.

Speaking of a long poem in the *Beppo* manner which he might write, Byron said, in a letter to John Murray dated March 25, 1818, "It will, at any rate, show them that I can write cheerfully, and repel the charge of monotony and mannerism."[3] And it was in this new mood of banter and irony that Byron commenced *Don Juan* in the autumn of the same year.

[2] Claude M. Fuess, in his *Lord Byron as a Satirist in Verse* (New York, 1912), p. 44, suggests that an even earlier poem contains a suggestion of the humorous, bantering spirit of the future *Don Juan*. He points to the poem, "To a Lady Who Presented to the Author a Lock of Hair Braided with His Own, and Appointed a Night in December to Meet Him in the Garden," which appeared in Byron's *Hours of Idleness* (1807).

[3] R. E. Prothero, *The Works of Lord Byron: Letters and Journals* (London, 1898–1902), IV, 217. (To John Murray. Venice, March 25, 1818.)

A detailed comparison of the early cantos of *Don Juan* with the later cantos of Byron's lengthy epic-satire reveals a striking and significant characteristic of the poem. Byron's *Don Juan* evinces definite growth. In the first five cantos the emphasis is primarily upon incident and the mood is sportively satirical. Byron finished Canto V in December 1820. He did not resume composition of the poem until June 1822. The cantos written after this long break in composition are more serious in tone, and the emphasis has shifted to social and political satire and revolutionary indoctrination. Let us make this pronounced shift in mood and emphasis the first subject of our inquiry.

Byron originally conceived of *Don Juan* as a sportive satire of the affectations and sophistries of society. On April 23, 1818, about four months before Byron began its first canto, he wrote to John Murray as follows:

I have something to say to . . . . the wretched affectations and systematized Sophistry of many men, women, and Children, now extant and absurd in and about London and elsewhere;— which and whom, in their false pretensions and nauseous attempts to make learning a nuisance and society a Bore, I consider as fair game—to be brought down on all fair occasions, and I doubt not, by the blessing of God on my honest purpose . . . . to extirpate, extinguish and eradicate such as come within the compass of my intention.[4]

It is reasonable to assume that Byron was thinking of another poem in the *Beppo* manner when he said this; and that poem was to be *Don Juan*.

Byron sounded the keynote of the first five cantos when, in announcing to Moore the completion of Canto I, he said, "It is called *Don Juan,* and is meant to be a little quietly facetious about everything."[5] Facetiousness, ban-

[4] Prothero, *op. cit.,* IV, 230. (To John Murray. Venice, April 23, 1818.)

[5] *Ibid.,* IV, 260. (To Thomas Moore. Venice, September 19, 1818.)

ter, and playfulness characterize the opening cantos of the poem.

Byron reiterated his sportive intention in a letter to Murray on August 12, 1819:

You are too earnest and eager about a work never intended to be serious. Do you suppose that I could have any intention but to giggle and make giggle?—a playful satire, with as little poetry as could be helped, was what I meant. . . .[6]

It is reasonable to suspect, however, that Byron is purposely minimizing the satiric element in his poem in order to disarm Murray's fears about publication. That Byron's major purpose in *Don Juan* from its very inception was satire of hypocrisy and cant is readily demonstrable. But there is a marked difference between the earlier and the later cantos in the quality of the satire, being more playful and less biting in the first five than in the subsequent ones.

In the opening cantos of *Don Juan* we find Byron joking about his lack of "design" and "regularity" of purpose, and emphasizing his playful, facetious, and mildly satirical intent. In Canto I, stanza vii, Byron speaks about "the regularity of my design" which "forbids all wandering as the worst of sinning." Again, in the same canto, he devotes three consecutive stanzas (ccvii–ccix) to a jocular discussion of his "moral" purpose.

In Canto IV, stanza v, Byron asserts:

> Some have accused me of a strange design
>   Against the creed and morals of the land,
> And trace it in this poem every line;
>   I don't pretend that I quite understand
> My own meaning when I would be *very* fine;
>   But the fact is that I have nothing plann'd,
> Unless it were to be a moment merry

. . . .

[6] Prothero, *op. cit.*, IV, 343. (To John Murray. Bologna, August 12, 1819.)

In the opening of the next canto (V, ii), Byron facetiously remarks that he will make his poem a "moral model":

> I therefore do denounce all amorous writing,
>   Except in such a way as not to attract;
> Plain—simple—short, and by no means inviting,
>   But with a moral to each error tack'd,
> Form'd rather for instructing than delighting,
>   And with all passions in their turn attack'd;
> Now, if my Pegasus should not be shod ill
> This poem will become a moral model.

While Byron's half-jesting claim here to be regarded as a moral teacher is not to be ignored, his purpose in these early cantos, we may reasonably assume, was predominantly jocular and gaily ironic rather than seriously satiric.

Turning now from Byron's own statements of his purpose to the subject matter of these cantos, we see that there is harmony between the two. In Canto I we have the amusing account of the genealogy of Don Juan, with its obviously autobiographical allusions and its thinly disguised portrait of Lady Byron. Then follows the description of the first of Juan's amours, the Julia episode. Canto II continues Juan's adventures, including his shipwreck and subsequent love affair with Haidée. In Cantos III and IV the passionate romance of Haidée and Juan comes to its tragic end and Juan is soon embroiled in the ludicrous seraglio escapade which occupies the whole of Canto V and is concluded in Canto VI.

As may be readily seen, the emphasis in these cantos, with the exception of the "Dedication," is upon incident. There is comparatively little of the speculative and satiric digression that abounds in the later cantos of the poem. The satiric element is subordinate to the interest in love and adventure. The dominant mood of these early cantos is one of bantering ridicule and gay profligacy.

II

THE SHIFT TO SOCIAL SATIRE AND REVO-LUTIONARY INDOCTRINATION

After Byron finished Canto V in December 1820 there ensued the longest of the several interruptions in the composition of *Don Juan*. Probably one of the factors in Byron's decision to discontinue the composition was the disapproval of Teresa Guiccioli. Byron had written the first two cantos of the poem before he met the Contessa in Venice in April 1819. It was after the publication of these cantos in July 1819 that Teresa first discovered the nature of the work. According to Lady Blessington's *Journal*, Teresa subsequently asked Byron to discontinue the poem because of its "immorality."[7] Teresa's reaction was merely the natural displeasure of a constant woman confronted with a cynical and jocular treatment of love. In October 1820, after he had begun the fifth canto, Byron wrote to his publisher: "At the particular request of the Countess G., I have promised *not* to continue *Don Juan*. You will therefore look upon these three cantos as the last of the poem."[8]

This might appear, at first sight, to be a deplorable interruption in Byron's composition of the poem. But it was after this break in composition that Byron's purpose and mood in *Don Juan* grew manifestly more serious. I am not aware that Teresa Guiccioli has been given any credit for the fact that the subsequent cantos were more serious and less open to moral criticism than their predecessors.

Byron composed Cantos VI, VII, and VIII during the period from June to August 8, 1822. In December of that

[7] Countess of Blessington, *A Journal of the Conversations of Lord Byron with the Countess of Blessington* (London, 1834), p. 206.

[8] R. E. Prothero, *The Works of Lord Byron: Letters and Journals* (London, 1898–1902), V, 320–21.

year he wrote a letter to Murray in which he voiced his increasing seriousness of satiric purpose in the poem: *"Don Juan* will be known by and bye, for what it is intended,— a *Satire* on *abuses* of the present states of Society . . . . "[9] This is evidence that, however uncertain he may have been originally as to the ultimate purpose of *Don Juan,* he was now committed to a definite objective.

In the later cantos we find Byron voicing again and again his increasing seriousness of purpose in his "epic satire." In stanza iii of the spirited opening of Canto VII he defends himself against those who claim his intention is to "scoff at human power and virtue":

> They accuse me—*Me*—the present writer of
> The present poem—of—I know not what—
> A tendency to under-rate and scoff
> At human power and virtue, and all that;
> And this they say in language rather rough.
> Good God! I wonder what they would be at!
> I say no more than hath been said in Dante's
> Verse, and by Solomon and by Cervantes;

He continues (stanza vii):

> Dogs, or men!—for I flatter you in saying
> That ye are dogs—your betters far—ye may
> Read or read not, what I am now essaying,
> To show ye what ye are in every way.

At the conclusion of Canto X (lxxxiv–lxxxv) Byron, addressing Englishmen, promises to tell them in the next canto truths they will not accept and warns them of his forthcoming attack upon English social abuses and hypocrisies:

[9] Prothero, *op. cit.,* VI, 155–56. (To John Murray. Genoa, December 25, 1822.)

He paused—and so will I; as doth a crew
  Before they give their broadside. By and by,
My gentle countrymen, we will renew
  Our old acquaintance; and at least I'll try
To tell you truths *you* will not take as true,
  Because they are so;—a male Mrs. Fry,
With a soft besom will I sweep your halls,
And brush a web or two from off the walls.

Oh Mrs. Fry! Why go to Newgate? Why
  Preach to poor rogues? And wherefore not begin
With Carlton, or with other houses? Try
  Your hand at harden'd and imperial sin.
To mend the people's an absurdity,
  A jargon, a mere philanthropic din,
Unless you make their betters better:—Fy!
I thought you had more religion, Mrs. Fry.[10]

And he concludes this warning of his promised satiric
attack with these words (X, lxxxvii):

. . . . I have prated
Just now enough; but by and by I'll prattle
Like Roland's horn in Roncesvalles' battle.

Again, in Canto XI (lxxxvii–lxxxviii) Byron reiterates
his satiric purpose in no uncertain words:

But how shall I relate in other cantos
  Of what befell our hero in the land,
Which 'tis the common cry and lie to vaunt as
  A moral country? But I hold my hand—
For I disdain to write an Atalantis;
  But 'tis as well at once to understand
You are *not* a moral people, and you know it
Without the aid of too sincere a poet.

[10] According to Janet Payne Whitney, author of the recent biography of Elizabeth Fry, the famous Quaker woman *did* preach at Carlton and other noble houses.

What Juan saw and underwent shall be
  My topic, with of course the due restriction
Which is required by proper courtesy;
  And recollect the work is only fiction,
And that I sing of neither mine nor me,
  Though every scribe, in some slight turn of
    diction,
Will hint allusions never *meant.* Ne'er doubt
This—when I speak, I *don't hint,* but *speak out.*

The seriousness of Byron's purpose becomes manifest in his extended and faithful picture of social abuses and affectations in these later cantos. In the following stanza (xl) from Canto XII Byron definitely avows his satiric purpose:

But now I'm going to be immoral; now
  I mean to show things really as they are,
Not as they ought to be: for I avow,
  That till we see what's what in fact, we're far
From much improvement with that virtuous plough
  Which skims the surface, leaving scarce a scar
Upon the black loam long manured by Vice,
Only to keep its corn at the old price.

Byron, acknowledging (XIV, xiii) that his poem is meeting with censure and contradiction, attributes the fact to its "too much truth":

Besides, my Muse by no means deals in fiction:
  She gathers a repertory of facts,
Of course with some reserve and slight restriction,
  But mostly sings of human things and acts—
And that's one cause she meets with contradiction;
  For too much truth, at first sight, ne'er attracts;
And were her object only what's call'd glory,
With more ease too she'd tell a different story.

For, Byron insinuates (XIV, xxii), there is a motive behind his choosing to say the unpopular thing, which may not be apparent to superficial readers:

> The grand arcanum's not for men to see all;
>   My music has some mystic diapasons;
> And there is much which could not be appreciated
> In any manner by the uninitiated.

Byron's iconoclastic intention is implied in the two ensuing stanzas (XIV, ci–cii):

> 'Tis strange,—but true; for truth is always strange;
>   Stranger than fiction: if it could be told,
> How much would novels gain by the exchange!
>   How differently the world would men behold!
> How oft would vice and virtue places change!
>   The new world would be nothing to the old,
> If some Columbus of the moral seas
> Would show mankind their souls' antipodes.
>
> What "antres vast and deserts idle" then
>   Would be discover'd in the human soul!
> What icebergs in the hearts of mighty men,
>   With self-love in the centre as their pole!
> What Anthropophagi are nine or ten
>   Of those who hold the kingdoms in control!
> Were things but only call'd by their right name,
> Caesar himself would be ashamed of fame.

One of the last, clearest, and most explicit of Byron's avowals of his serious moral purpose and satiric intent occurs in Canto XV (xcii–xciii):

> But though I am a temperate theologian,
>   And also meek as a metaphysician,
> Impartial between Tyrian and Trojan
>   As Eldon on a lunatic commission,
> In politics my duty is to show John
>   Bull something of the lower world's condition.

It makes my blood boil like the springs of Hecla,
To see men let these scoundrel sovereigns break law.

But politics, and policy, and piety,
  Are topics which I sometimes introduce,
Not only for the sake of their variety,
  But as subservient to a moral use;
Because my business is to *dress* society,
  And stuff with *sage* that very verdant goose.

These avowals of purpose, explicit or implied, constitute, I believe, sufficient evidence to establish the increased
seriousness of Byron's purpose in the later cantos of *Don
Juan*. When we come to examine the subject matter of
these cantos we shall find that Byron's statement of purpose and his poetic performance coincide.

It is advisable, now, to look for a moment at Byron's
political views and to observe the conditions under which
they were formed in order that we may better understand
the motives behind his emphasis upon political and social
satire and revolutionary indoctrination. The background
of Byron's political interests during the period from his
Cambridge days to his taking his seat in the House of
Lords has been summarized as follows:

After two previous attacks of insanity, George III became
permanently demented in 1810, and the Regency Bill, making
Prince George actual ruler of the nation, was passed on February
5, 1810. His [the Regent's] well-known vicious propensities
and illicit amours had made him unpopular, and when, on February 23, 1812, he first appeared in public as sovereign, he was
coldly received. It had been generally supposed that with the
power in his hands, he would reward the Whigs who had stood
by him so faithfully through his many difficulties, but after vain
efforts to organize a coalition ministry, he appointed Lord Liverpool as Prime Minister on June 9, 1812, and the Tories retained
complete control over affairs of state. This action, equivalent to
treachery, made the Regent a target for Whig abuse, and that

party never ceased reviling the ruler who had been disloyal to their cause. Byron at Cambridge had rather lukewarmly supported Whig doctrines, and when he took his seat in the House of Lords, he selected one of the neutral benches.[11]

Later, when he took up his residence in London, Byron allied himself with the Whigs. This alignment of himself with the more liberal and progressive party is quite understandable in view of his independent temperament and liberal inclinations. Then, too, Byron's association with Leigh Hunt, Thomas Moore, and other liberal thinkers and writers may have assisted his espousal of liberal views. Once he had identified himself with the cause of political liberalism he soon became a leader of those who insisted on liberty of speech and action. ". . . . It is necessary," he wrote to Moore, "in the present clash of philosophy and tyranny, to throw away the scabbard. I know it is against fearful odds; but the battle must be fought; and it will be eventually for the good of mankind, whatever it may be for the individual who risks himself."[12] And again Byron expressed his devotion to liberty in these words: "There are but two sentiments to which I am constant,—a strong love of liberty and a detestation of cant."[13]

It was this strong love of liberty and detestation of cant that moved Byron to write the vigorous preface to Cantos VI, VII, and VIII of *Don Juan,* in which, in no uncertain terms, he inveighed against the "notorious abuses of the name of God and the mind of man." From this preface I quote the following pertinent passage:

The hackneyed and lavished title of Blasphemer—which, with Radical, Liberal, Jacobin, Reformer, &c., are the changes which the hirelings are daily ringing in the ears of those who will

---

[11] Fuess, *op. cit.,* pp. 94 ff. Quoted by permission of Columbia University Press, publishers.

[12] Prothero, *op. cit.,* VI, 101. (To Thomas Moore. Pisa, August 8, 1822.)   [13] Blessington, *op. cit.,* p. 390.

listen—should be welcome to all who recollect on *whom* it was originally bestowed. Socrates and Jesus Christ were put to death publicly as *blasphemers*, and so have been and may be many who dare to oppose the most notorious abuses of the name of God and the mind of man.[14]

This preface was Byron's battle cry before he took up the cudgels against religious, political, and social abuses and hypocrisies in the later cantos of *Don Juan*. He re-echoed the cry in the powerful language of the following stanza (IX, xxiv):

And I will war, at least in words (and—should
　My chance so happen—deeds), with all who war
With Thought;—and of Thought's foes by far most rude,
　Tyrants and sycophants have been and are.
I know not who may conquer: if I could
　Have such a prescience, it should be no bar
To this my plain, sworn, downright detestation
Of every despotism in every nation.

In commencing his attack, Byron first applies his principles to current problems of British politics. He condemns the English foreign policy of acquiescence in the efforts of Continental powers to oppose reforms and stifle liberty. He condemns obnoxious domestic measures. And he questions the integrity of English statesmen whom he considers responsible for England's domestic and foreign difficulties. The later cantos of *Don Juan* bristle with satire of social and political abuses, British foreign policy, statesmen, diplomats, and military heroes. Byron's ultimate objective in all this criticism of England and things English appears to be to show how imperfect is the boasted freedom and morality of England.

But Byron does not by any means confine his ridicule to England. He avowed his "detestation" of "despotism

[14] Byron's *Poetical Works* (Oxford University Press, 1928), p. 717.

in every nation." And he exerted the full strength of his
satiric power against the prevailing spirit of oppression and
reactionary conservatism which, following Napoleon's
overthrow, was permeating Europe. It was Byron who
may be said to have originated the radical campaign against
European political romanticism and against the Holy Alliance which, as Brandes has rightly said, was "nothing but
a systematization of the political hypocrisy of Europe."[15]
After Napoleon's defeat, the governments of Europe ar-
rayed themselves in opposition to reforms and sought to
stifle the newly achieved freedom of the masses. They
sought every means of arresting progress; they clung
blindly and tenaciously to outworn institutions, and made
every effort to rehabilitate them. The Holy Alliance
forgot the promises given to the nations and endeavored
to deprive them by force of their right to self-government.
The inevitable result was an increasing passion throughout
Europe for a radical revolution. With this strong under-
current Byron identified his powerful poetic expression.
In short, in *Don Juan* Byron became the poet of the crisis.
"Free, in his quality of English peer, from molestation
anywhere, he made himself the mouthpiece of the dumb
revolutionary indignation which was seething in the breasts
of the best friends and lovers of liberty in Europe."[16]

In his life as in his poetry, Byron identified himself
with the oppressed. He risked his life and his fortune in
the short-lived Italian attempt for freedom (1820–1821)
and he gave both his fortune and his life in the cause of
Greek liberty (1823–1824). "I am become," he once said
to Medwin, "a citizen of the world."[17] "There is nothing

[15] George Brandes, *Main Currents in Nineteenth-Century Literature*
(London, 1901–1905), IV, 355.
[16] *Ibid.*, p. 356.
[17] Thomas Medwin, *Journal of the Conversations of Lord Byron,
Noted During a Residence with his Lordship at Pisa, in the Years 1821
and 1822* (London, 1824), pp. 282–83.

left for Mankind but a Republic," he wrote in his *Journal* in 1821, "and I think that there are hopes of such. The two Americas . . . . have it; Spain and Portugal approach it; all thirst for it. Oh Washington!"[18] "A Republic" it was that Byron hoped for. And he saw no way of bringing it about except revolution. He gives clear and decisive expression to this conviction in stanzas l–li of Canto VIII:

> But never mind;—"God save the king!" and kings!
>   For if *he* don't, I doubt if *men* will longer—
> I think I hear a little bird, who sings
>   The people by and by will be the stronger:
> The veriest jade will wince whose harness wrings
>   So much into the raw as quite to wrong her
> Beyond the rules of posting,—and the mob
> At last fall sick of imitating Job.
>
> At first it grumbles, then it swears, and then,
>   Like David, flings smooth pebbles 'gainst a giant;
> At last it takes to weapons such as men
>   Snatch when despair makes human hearts less pliant.
> Then comes the "tug of war;"—'twill come again,
>   I rather doubt; and I would fain say "fie on't,"
> If I had not perceived that revolution
> Alone can save the earth from hell's pollution.

The quotations from the later cantos which I now present are, it seems to me, conclusive evidence of Byron's genuine revolutionary fervor and of his radical indoctrination.[19] That Byron was well aware of the potency and widespread influence of liberal poetry is evidenced in these words from stanza xciii of Canto VI:

---

[18] "Detached Thoughts, No. 112," in *The Ravenna Journal* (Longmans, Green and Co., Inc., London, 1928), p. 94.

[19] Additional evidence is Byron's "The Vision of Judgment" (1821) and the apostrophe to freedom in *Childe Harold* (IV, xcviii).

> . . . . and now rhymes wander
> Almost as far as Petersburgh, and lend
> A dreadful impulse to each loud meander
> Of murmuring Liberty's wide waves, which blend
> Their roar even with the Baltic's—

He strikes a direct blow at the traitorous efforts of the Holy Alliance to crush "young Freedom," and he prophesies (VII, lxxix) that the reactionary European governments "will not find Liberty a Troy!"

> Oh, thou eternal Homer! who couldst charm
> All ears, though long; all ages, though so short,
> By merely wielding with poetic arm
> Arms to which men will never more resort,
> Unless gunpowder should be found to harm
> Much less than is the hope of every court,
> Which now is leagued young Freedom to annoy;
> But they will not find Liberty a Troy:—

In the openings stanzas (iii–iv) of Canto VIII, Byron defends war that is fought for freedom—"freedom's battles"—and condemns all other war. Stanza v continues:

> Not so Leonidas and Washington,
> Whose every battle-field is holy ground,
> Which breathes of nations saved, not worlds undone.
> How sweetly on the ear such echoes sound!
> While the mere victor's may appal or stun
> The servile and the vain, such names will be
> A watchword till the future shall be free.

And Byron does not intend to sit idly by waiting for "the future" to "be free." He means to lend his strong voice to the hastening of that consummation; as stanzas cxxxv and cxxxvii put it:

> For I will teach, if possible, the stones
> To rise against earth's tyrants. Never let it
> Be said that we still truckle unto thrones;—

But ye—our children's children! think how we
Show'd *what things were* before the world was free!

.   .   .   .

And when you hear historians talk of thrones,
    And those that sate upon them, let it be
As we now gaze upon the mammoth's bones,
    And wonder what old world such things could see,
Or hieroglyphics on Egyptian stones,
    The pleasant riddles of futurity—
Guessing at what shall happily be hid,
As the real purpose of a pyramid.

In the following lines Byron's condemnation of oppression rises to indubitable revolutionary exhortation. He
denounces kings as "spiders" and their ministers as "human
insects, catering for spiders" (IX, xxvii), and then (xxviii)
he cries:

Raise but an arm! 'twill brush their web away,
    And without *that,* their poison and their claws
Are useless. Mind, good people! what I say—
    (Or rather peoples)—*go on* without pause!
The web of these tarantulas each day
    Increases, till you shall make common cause:
None, save the Spanish fly and Attic bee,
As yet are strongly stinging to be free.

This is the most incendiary of Byron's many radical
utterances in the later cantos of *Don Juan.*

The next utterance (XI, xxvii) is less vigorous but
pregnant with suggestion. Byron hints to the English,
apropos of the French Revolution, that gentlemen sus-
pended from lampposts and bonfires made of country-
seats "may illuminate mankind."

A row of gentlemen along the streets
    Suspended, may illuminate mankind,
As also bonfires made of country-seats;

Toward the end of Canto XII (lxxxiii) Byron declares that "constitutional possession" of a throne is the only justifiable kingship, but adds that even this is but a step in the inevitable "progression of freedom" which shall complete the education of despots.

The quotations with which I conclude this discussion reveal most clearly the essence of Byron's doctrine of freedom. "Born for opposition" (XV, xxii), as he describes himself, he always allies himself with "the weaker side" (xxiii):

> But then 'tis mostly on the weaker side;
>   So that I verily believe if they
> Who now are basking in their full-blown pride
>   Were shaken down and "dogs had had their day,"
> Though at the first I might perchance deride
>   Their tumble, I should turn the other way,
> And wax an ultra-royalist in loyalty,
> Because I hate even democratic royalty.

He wishes (IX, xxv) men to be free "as much from mobs as kings":

> It is not that I adulate the people:
>   Without *me*, there are demagogues enough,
> And infidels, to pull down every steeple,
>   And set up in their stead some proper stuff.
> Whether they may sow scepticism to reap hell,
>   As is the Christian dogma rather rough,
> I do not know;—I wish men to be free
> As much from mobs as kings—from you as me.

In short, these later cantos of *Don Juan* are Lord Byron's protest against all oppression, whether of tyrants or mobs. They are Byron's protest against all that hampers individual freedom or interferes with true independence. In marked contrast to the sportive mood of the earlier cantos, the later cantos emphasize serious political and social satire, and Byron becomes a trumpet voice, a leading exponent of that immense social movement of the early nineteenth century which we distinguish as "the Revolution."

III

THE FACTORS

What were the factors which contributed to Byron's increasing seriousness during the period from December 1820, when he broke off the composition of *Don Juan*, to June 1822, when he resumed his composition of the poem? A careful examination of Byron's life, letters, journals, works, and reading and an equally careful examination of the political and social events of the period produce no startling or extraordinary revelations. But they do support the opinion that Byron's increased seriousness is but the inevitable and natural result of his attainment of spiritual and creative maturity. Byron's seriousness in these cantos is not a sudden and inexplicable innovation. Almost from the first, Byron sought expression in satire because the satiric spirit was one of the fundamental elements of his nature. His early satires, coarsely and bluntly personal and often violent and abusive in tone, were in the manner and mood of the neoclassic satiric tradition of Pope and Dryden. However, as Byron's satiric genius developed, it tended to employ less and less of the traditional axe-swinging of the neoclassic satirists and to approach more and more the mocking and ironic manner of the Italian burlesque poets. This is best exemplified in *Beppo* and in the earlier cantos of *Don Juan*. Finally, when his satiric genius had fully ripened, Byron found complete expression in the serious political and social satire of the later cantos of *Don Juan*.

Satire was Byron's natural and habitual response to

censure and injury. When, as a youth, he was wounded by the severity of the criticism of his *Hours of Idleness* (1807), he responded angrily in *English Bards and Scotch Reviewers* (1809). In Italy in 1819, banished from his native country and ostracized by English society, Byron's sense of injury was deep and acute. Again his reaction was satire. True, he began *Don Juan* in the sportively satirical mood of the Italian burlesque poets. But as the months and years of exile passed, and insult and calumny were added to ostracism by a "morally outraged" society, Byron's rankling resentment against "the degraded and hypocritical mass which leavens the present English generation"[20] deepened, and finally in the later cantos of *Don Juan*, he inveighed against all the most flagrant abuses of his cant-ridden age.

I should like to suggest some of the factors which may have contributed to the maturation of Byron's satiric genius and, hence, to the growth of *Don Juan*.

The influence of Teresa Guiccioli upon Byron has never been adequately recognized and appreciated. Attention needs to be called to the salutary nature of her influence in general upon Byron's health, morals, and genius. This woman definitely influenced Byron's life during the period of the composition of the major part of his most significant work, *Don Juan*. She has suffered much at the hands of certain critics. But the worst of their accusations are merely that she had an exaggerated notion of Byron's affection for her and that she disapproved of *Don Juan* and urged him to discontinue it. The first accusation is invalidated by Byron's avowals of his affection for her, the sincerity of which there is no reason to doubt. We have the authentic testimony of his intimate associates during this period concerning his conduct toward and his statements about

[20] Byron's Preface to Cantos VI, VII, and VIII in his *Poetical Works* (Oxford University Press, 1928), p. 717.

Teresa.[21] The substance of this evidence is that in Teresa Guiccioli Byron found at last a generous, loyal, sympathetic, understanding friend and a devoted and affectionate companion. His passionate heart, always seeking for that better love which heretofore had eluded him, found center and balance in the true love of a true woman. Teresa's love was a stabilizing influence just when Byron's emotions most needed stabilizing. For Teresa, Byron permanently abandoned libertinism and, thereafter, confined and directed his energies to poetic production.

As for the second charge, it becomes a point in Teresa's favor when properly viewed. At her request Byron discontinued the composition of *Don Juan*, and with her permission he resumed composition. When, in July 1822, Byron wrote Murray that he had obtained permission from Teresa to continue the work provided that it be more guarded and serious in the continuation than in the beginning,[22] there was soberness of intention beneath his surface levity.

That Teresa's concern may have been a factor in the increased seriousness of the later cantos of *Don Juan* has been ignored by most, if not all, of Byron critics and biographers. But this neglect of Teresa's influence is but a part of the usual tendency to minimize the importance of her general influence upon Lord Byron. This tendency is one which, I am convinced, is entirely unwarranted by all the evidence. Teresa understood and sympathized with Byron's motives in his serious satire of society and politics in the later cantos of *Don Juan*. Her own estimate of the significance and worth of the poem manifests extraordinary

[21] Thomas Moore, *The Life, Letters, and Journals of Lord Byron* (London, 1908), pp. 393, 402, 406–7, 469; Thomas Medwin, *Journal of the Conversations of Lord Byron, 1821–1822* (London, 1824), pp. 20, 319–20; Blessington, *op. cit.*, pp. 115–16.

[22] Prothero, *op. cit.*, VI, 95. (To John Murray. Pisa, July 8, 1822.)

discernment and generous appreciation.[23] Byron respected the opinion of this eminently sensible woman.

There were several events during this period of interruption in the composition of *Don Juan* which may well have contributed to the growth of Byron's seriousness. This period witnessed the distressing trouble with Claire Clairmont over Allegra, the death of Allegra, the "Cain" outcry, and the quarrels with Murray which led, eventually, to Byron's change of publishers.[24] Ethel C. Mayne is of the opinion that the Pisan period (November 1821–September 1822) is "the most utterly saddening of his career. There is nothing to struggle with, nothing to resign."[25] This period included also the death of Byron's fellow poet, Shelley, in the Bay of Lerici in July 1822.

Byron's letters during the period from December 1820 to June 1822 manifest the gradually increasing seriousness which characterizes all his correspondence from the time of his arrival in Italy to his death in Greece. But even more noteworthy in this respect are his diaries and journals during this period. I refer here to several entries in a journal which Byron began in Ravenna in May 1821 and concluded in May 1822.[26] In "Detached Thoughts, No. 96," Byron's mind dwells long and seriously on the nature of the human soul and the probability of its immortality, and he concludes that "Man is born *passionate* of body, but with an innate though secret tendency to the love of Good in his Mainspring of Mind." In the next entry, "Detached Thoughts, No. 97," he speculates upon the nature of Reality and suggests the plausibility of "Mind"

[23] Teresa Guiccioli, *My Recollections of Lord Byron* (New York, 1869).

[24] Ethel C. Mayne, *Byron* (London, 1924), pp. 360–90.

[25] *Ibid.*, p. 381.

[26] *The Ravenna Journal* (edited by Lord Ernle, London, 1928), pp. 19 ff.

being as eternal as "Matter." "I have often been inclined to Materialism in philosophy," he says in "Detached Thoughts, No. 98," "but could never bear its introduction into *Christianity*, which appears to me essentially founded upon the *Soul*. . . . . I own my partiality for *Spirit*."

What was Byron reading during this period? His reading, for the most part, does not differ essentially from his habitual reading. He read Scott's novels, of which he had said, "I like no reading better," several Gothic novels, Lamb's *Specimens*, and Milton's *Comus*. Reading indicating more serious inclinations included Johnson's *Vanity of Human Wishes*,[27] the Bible,[28] and Burton's *Anatomy of Melancholy*.[29] Byron was also re-reading the works of Henry Fielding. He observed that "the inequality of conditions, and the littleness of the great, were never set forth in stronger terms" than in Fielding's novels, and that were Fielding living he would be denounced as a mouthpiece of the revolutionists.[30] Byron and Fielding seem very much alike in their detestation of cant and hypocrisy. In his preface to *Joseph Andrews* Fielding announced a design of "A Comic Epic Poem in Prose."[31] Perhaps Byron thought of turning it back into poetry again. At least one might almost describe *Don Juan* (except for Byron's self-portraiture) as Fielding in verse applied to a different age. *Don Juan* bears a striking resemblance in general tone and manner to the novels of Fielding, particularly *Tom Jones*, *Joseph Andrews*, and *Jonathan Wild*. It may be significant that Byron was thinking of Fielding and re-reading him. Byron wrote in his journal in the late fall of 1821:

[27] Prothero, *op. cit.*, V, 161.   [28] *Ibid.*, V, 391–92.
[29] *Loc. cit.*
[30] *The Ravenna Journal*, "Detached Thoughts, No. 116," p. 96.
[31] Henry Fielding, *The Adventures of Joseph Andrews* . . . .
(London, 1910), pp. xxv–xliv.

I have lately been reading Fielding over again. They talk of Radicalism, Jacobinism, etc., in England (I am told), but they should turn over the pages of *Jonathan Wild the Great.* The inequality of conditions, and the littleness of the great, were never set forth in stronger terms . . . . And yet I never recollect to have heard this turn of Fielding's mind noticed, though it is obvious in every page.[32]

In other words, Byron recognized in Fielding a kindred spirit, one who like himself delighted in exposing social abuses and in ridiculing affectation and hypocrisy.

It should also be remarked that during this period Byron was intimately associated with Shelley at Pisa. Shelley's seriousness and his ardent, revolutionary radicalism undoubtedly exerted a decided influence upon Byron.

Both Shelley and Byron were alert to the political events which were taking place in the world around them during this time. There were numerous insurrections in 1820–1822 in Spain, Portugal, Naples, Greece, and South America. Everywhere "Young Freedom" was rankling under the recently reforged shackles of "Legitimacy."[33] The European Powers were doing their utmost to suppress insurrections. "There is nothing left for Mankind but a Republic, and I think that there are hopes of such," Byron wrote in October 1821.[34] His beloved Greece was beginning her determined struggle for freedom. Revolt against oppression was in the air, and Byron was soon to attain his full stature as a strong champion, in both word and deed, of human freedom.

Finally, several of Byron's other works written during this period attest his increasing inclination toward social

[32] "Detached Thoughts, No. 116," *The Ravenna Journal,* p. 96.
[33] Ferdinand Schevill, *A History of Europe* (New York, 1930), pp. 467–78.
[34] "Detached Thoughts, No. 112," *The Ravenna Journal,* p. 94.

satire and revolutionary indoctrination. *Cain, The Vision of Judgment, The Blues,* and *The Irish Avatar* were written during this time, and it was not many months after his resumption of *Don Juan* in June 1822 that Byron began his concentrated satiric attack upon the political and social abuses of his age in *The Age of Bronze* (December 1822).

In conclusion, these several factors which I have enumerated I believe contributed to Byron's increasing soberness of purpose during the period from December 1820 to June 1822. The growth of *Don Juan* in satiric seriousness is but the natural consequence of Byron's attainment of spiritual and creative maturity. In the later cantos of *Don Juan* we witness the flowering of Byron's essentially satiric genius.

Chapter Two

THE CONTEMPORARY REVIEWS
OF *DON JUAN*

I

THE REVIEWS

THE contemporary reception in England of Byron's epic social satire is nowhere better revealed than in the periodical reviews of Byron's day. It is my purpose to present here the reviews of *Don Juan* which appeared in the English periodicals from August 1819 to April 1824, to appraise them in the light of the dominant critical prejudices of the period, and to determine their effect upon Byron.

Samuel C. Chew, in his penetrating and comprehensive study of Byron's reputation, *Byron in England, His Fame and After Fame*, includes a thorough review of the pamphleteer criticism of *Don Juan* and of the *Don Juan* continuations and aprocrypha.[1] For this reason I have excluded the pamphleteer criticism from consideration in this study and have confined my attention exclusively to the periodical reviews.

In presenting the reviews of *Don Juan* I have quoted in each case representative passages which illustrate the tone of the review, following the excerpt with a summary of the substance of the entire article.

As Professor Chew relates, for several days prior to the

---

[1] Samuel C. Chew, *Byron in England, His Fame and After Fame* (London, 1924), pp. 27 ff.

appearance of *Don Juan* the English newspapers printed
the mysterious and arresting advertisement: "In a few
days—*Don Juan.*" On July 15, 1819, Cantos I and II
appeared, without the name of author or publisher. The
poem was greeted with immediate praise and censure. The
journals were divided. The more liberal ventured to support Byron. The *Edinburgh Review* and the *Quarterly*
remained silent. *Blackwood's* led the attack, inveighing
chiefly against the immorality of the poem:

. . . . That Lord Byron has never written anything more
decisively and triumphantly expressive of the greatness of his
genius, will be allowed by all who have read the poem. That
(laying for a moment all its manifold and grievous offences out
of our view) it is by far the most admirable specimen of the
mixture of ease, strength, gaiety, and seriousness extant in the
whole body of English poetry, is a proposition to which, we are
almost as well persuaded, very few of them will refuse their
assent. With sorrow and humiliation do we speak it—the poet
has devoted his powers to the worst of purposes and passions. . . . .
The moral strain of the whole poem is pitched in the lowest
key—and if the genius of the author lifts him now and then out
of his pollution, it seems as if he regretted the elevation, and
made all haste to descend again. . . . . It appears, in short, as if
this miserable man, having exhausted every species of sensual
gratification—having drained the cup of sin even to its bitterest
dregs, were resolved to show us that he is no longer a human
being, even in his frailties;—but a cool, unconcerned fiend
laughing with a detestable glee over the whole of the better and
worse elements of which human life is composed—treating well-
nigh with equal derision the most pure of virtues, and the most
odious of vices—dead alike to the beauty of the one and the deformity of the other, a mere heartless despiser of that frail but
noble humanity, whose type was never exhibited in a shape of
more deplorable degradation than in his own contemptuously distinct delineation of himself. . . . . Impiously railing against his
God—madly and meanly disloyal to his Sovereign and his coun-

try,—and brutally outraging all the best feelings of female
honour, affection, and confidence . . . . [It is scarcely believ-
able] that the odious malignity of this man's bosom should have
carried him so far as to make him commence a filthy and impious
poem, with an elaborate satire on the character and manners of
his wife—from whom, even by his own confession, he has been
separated only in consequence of his own cruel and heartless mis-
conduct. . . . . Lady Byron, however, has one consolation still
remaining, and yet we fear she will think it but a poor one. She
shares the scornful satire of her husband, not only with all that is
good, and pure, and high, in human nature,—its principles and
its feelings; but with every individual also, in whose character
the predominance of these blessed elements has been sufficient to
excite the envy, or exacerbate the despair of this guilty man . . . .
But our indignation, in regard to the morality of the poem, has
not blinded us to its manifold beauties . . . .[2]

Here is high praise mingled with severe censure. To
recapitulate the strictures of the *Blackwood's* reviewer:
the poem is the most intense infusion of genius and vice,
power and profligacy, that has appeared in any poem written in the English or any other modern language; wickedness is inextricably mingled with the beauty, grace, and
strength of a most inimitable and incomprehensible muse;
it must of necessity take a high place in English literature
and remain a perpetual monument of the "exalted intellect" and "depraved heart" of its author; it represents
the highest expression of Byron's genius; and it is the
most admirable specimen of the mixture of ease, strength,
gaiety, and seriousness in English poetry.

These great powers, the reviewer laments, are devoted

[2] *"Don Juan.* Cantos I–II," in *Blackwood's Edinburgh Magazine,*
V (August 1819), 512–18. *Blackwood's* was Tory in politics. John
Wilson ("Christopher North"), James Hogg, and John Gibson Lock-
hart were among the leading writers for the magazine at this time. See
Walter Graham, *English Literary Periodicals* (New York, 1930), pp.
230 and 275.

to the worst of purposes and passions; the moral strain is
of the lowest; love, honor, patriotism, and religion are
scoffed at and derided; "this miserable man" is no longer
human, even in his frailties, but a cool, unconcerned fiend,
laughingly equalizing virtues and vices—a mere heartless
despiser of frail humanity, laying bare the hidden con-
vulsions and abominable thoughts of a wicked spirit and
doing this with the calm ferociousness of satisfied de-
pravity, without hesitation, contrition, or remorse.

The author, he continues, is obviously devoid of religion; his faith is but momentary and not of the heart; he
scorns the better part of woman, and thus his love poetry
is an insult to love; he is impious toward God, disloyal
to his King; and he brutally outrages female honor, affection, and confidence.

The reviewer then attacks Byron virulently for commencing his "filthy and impious" poem with "an elaborate
satire on the character and manners of his wife." He en-
joins Lady Byron to take comfort in the knowledge that
her husband attacks *all* individuals of good and pure and
high character.

The critic concludes his review with his illustrations of
the "manifold beauties" of the poem. He quotes the description of Juan's ancestry, the description of Julia, the
moonlight scene of the two young lovers Juan and Julia,
Julia's tirade against her husband, and Julia's letter. He
praises the idyllic love of Juan and Haidée but calls it the
"same game of guilt and abandonment." And, finally, he
lauds the description of the shipwreck, avowing that it is
superior to the *Aeneid*. Clearly this Tory review is motivated not only by political bias but also by religious fear
and bigotry. The reviews of this time were extremely concerned about religious and political defection. Byron had
allied himself with the Whigs and had been accused of
atheism.

The British Critic followed suit with a disparaging review of the two cantos, in which the poem was not only
charged with immorality but was denied any literary excellence.[3] The reviewer begins with an ironic account of the
mystification that preceded the appearance of *Don Juan:*

Some unusual exertion was necessary to recover the waning
admiration of the public. A Satire was accordingly announced,
in terms so happily mysterious, as to set the town on the very
tiptoe of expectation. A thousand low and portentous murmurs
preceded its birth. At one time it was declared to be so intolerably severe, that an alarming increase was to be apprehended in
the catalogue of our national suicides—at another, it was stated
to be of a complexion so blasphemous, as even in these days of
liberality, to endanger the personal security of the bookseller.—
The trade, it was whispered, had shrunk back one by one, from
all the splendid temptations which attended its publication.—Paternoster-row was paralysed . . . . Fearful indeed was the
prodigy—a book without a book-seller; an advertisement without
an advertiser—"a deed without a name." After all this portentous parturition, out creeps *Don Juan*—and, doubtless, much
to the general disappointment of the town, as innocent of satire,
as any other Don in the Spanish dominions.[4]

The reviewer then asserts that the versification is on a
par with the morality:

If *Don Juan* then be not a satire—what is it? . . . . not a
tittle could, even in the utmost latitude of interpretation, be dignified by the name of poetry. It has not wit enough to be comic;
it has not spirit enough to make it lyric; nor is it didactic of anything but mischief. The versification and morality are about
upon a par; as far therefore as we are enabled to give it any
character at all, we should pronounce it a narrative of degrading
debauchery in doggrel rhyme . . . .[5]

[3] *"Don Juan,* I–II," in *The British Critic,* XII (August 1819),
196–204. *The British Critic* was Tory in politics. T. F. Middleton
and W. R. Lyall conducted it at this time. Cf. Graham, *op. cit.,* p. 221.
      [4] *Ibid.,* p. 196.   [5] *Ibid.,* pp. 197–204.

The most obvious difference between the review in *Blackwood's* and this review is that the former praises highly the poetic power and genius which the poem manifests while the latter denies the poem any poetic value. Noteworthy also is *The British Critic*'s categorical accusation of deliberate intention on the part of Byron to recommend, encourage, and "afford practical hints" for the consummation of adultery. The critic characterizes the poem as "a narrative of degrading debauchery in doggrel rhyme"; the adventures of a common man, ill-conceived, tedious, and poorly written; a composition bad in taste, feeling, expression, and heart, without wit and spirit; a shamelessly indecent "manual of profligacy," the purpose of which is to make vice alluring.

There is in this review but this slight modicum of praise: the reviewer admits that in the incidents and character there is a broad, boisterous, and "quite irresistible" humor which provokes "free and hearty laughter." This review, appearing like the first in a Tory journal, is clearly illustrative of the moral hypocrisy or "cant" so characteristic of the reviews of the period.

The Eclectic Review reiterated *The British Critic*'s charge of Byron's deliberate intention to corrupt and to seduce. These remarks occur in a review[6] of Lord Byron's *Mazeppa* in which *Don Juan* is not mentioned by name.

. . . . Poetry which it is impossible to read without admiration, yet which it is equally impossible to admire without losing some degree of self respect; such as no brother could read aloud to his sister; no husband to his wife;—poetry in which the deliberate purpose of the Author is to corrupt by inflaming the mind, to seduce to the love of evil which he has himself chosen as his

---

[6] *"Mazeppa,"* in *The Eclectic Review,* XII (August 1819), 147–56. *The Eclectic Review* was a sectarian religious organ of the Dissenters. Its insignificant literary criticism remains anonymous. Cf. Graham, *op. cit.,* p. 239.

good; can be safely dealt with only in one way, by passing it over in silence . . . .

These lines, which we wish to redeem from the profane ribaldry of their context, are exceedingly touching, and they have that character of truth which distinguishes Lord Byron's poetry. He writes like a man who has that clear perception of the truth of things, which is the result of the guilty knowledge of good and evil, and who, by the light of that knowledge, has deliberately preferred the evil, with a proud malignity of purpose which would seem to leave little for the last consummating change to accomplish. When he calculates that the reader is on the verge of pitying him, he takes care to throw him back the defiance of laughter, as if to let him know that all the Poet's pathos is but the sentimentalism of the drunkard between his cups, or the relenting softness of the courtesan, who the next moment resumes the bad boldness of her degraded character. With such a man who would wish either to laugh or to weep? And yet, who that reads him, can refrain alternately from either?

The Eclectic Review agrees with *The British Critic* that Byron has deliberately and maliciously chosen evil as his good; but *The Eclectic Review*, unlike *The British Critic*, is not blind to the poetic beauty of the poem—"Poetry which it is impossible to read without admiration . . . ." The reviewer finds passages which are moving and which have "that character of truth which distinguishes Lord Byron's poetry." Furthermore, the *Eclectic* reviewer deserves credit for remarking one of Byron's most pronounced characteristics in *Don Juan*, his promptness to throw back the "defiance of laughter" the moment he perceives the reader to be "on the verge of pitying him." In the main, however, this review is motivated by the religious bigotry which characterized a sectarian religious organ of that day.

The Gentleman's Magazine, in a brief notice of Byron's latest poem, lamented the prostitution of such high talents to infidelity and libertinism:

This work which has been so mysteriously announced for some time, has at length been given to the Publick . . . . it is obviously intended as a Satire upon some of the conspicuous characters of the day. . . . . *Don Juan* is ascribed to a nobleman whose poetical vigour and fertility have raised him into the highest rank of modern Bards. But the best friends of the Poet must, with ourselves, lament to observe abilities of so high an order rendered subservient to the spirit of infidelity and libertinism, so evidently manifested throughout the whole. The Noble Bard, by employing his genius on a worthy subject, might delight and instruct mankind; but the present work, though written with ease and spirit, and containing many truly poetical passages, cannot be read by persons of moral and religious feelings without the most decided reprobation and contempt.[7]

Like *Blackwood's, The Gentleman's Magazine* deplores the devotion of high powers to low purposes. According to it, the poem, though written with ease and spirit and containing passages of true poetry, is permeated with the spirit of infidelity and libertinism. It is noteworthy that the reviewer in *The Gentleman's Magazine* takes cognizance of Byron's satiric purpose in the poem. Although political prejudice is not operative in this criticism, it is apparent that alarm about Byron's defection from religious conservatism supplies the motivation.

The next review from which I quote denies Byron even the refuge of satire. This appeared in the *New Monthly Magazine*.[8]

I pass on to his satire. . . . . Misanthropy is very satirical, and

---

[7] *"Don Juan.* I–II," in *The Gentleman's Magazine*, LXXXIX (August 1819), 152. John Nichols was editor of the magazine at this time. Its contributors were legion. Cf. Graham, *op. cit.*, pp. 158–60.

[8] *"Don Juan.* I–II," in *New Monthly Magazine*, November 1, 1819, p. 381. The *New Monthly Magazine* had been founded in 1814 as a definitely political organ, with the counteracting of the Jacobinism of the *Monthly Magazine* as its precise aim. Henry Colburn was its editor until 1820. Cf. Graham, *op. cit.*, pp. 284–85.

I know no work of Lord Byron's that may not properly be termed a satire on religion, morality, social order, or domestic feeling; but *his satire is not satire;* it is only the morbid effusion of universal misanthropy. He lashes not with the hope of causing amendment, but of inflicting pain: the arm is strong, and the scourge is heavy; but there is no benefit in the blow . . . .

The reviewer then descends to vituperation:

> Crime itself appears too vapid for his taste; simple fornication is not enough, it must be seasoned by adultery, by incest, by every loathsome, and ineffable combination. Vice, in its unmodified state, is not sufficiently meretricious. The harlot must be arrayed in the tempting and transparent splendor of the Coa vestimenta. The Priapus must be attired in full-dress, drawers of the thinnest silk to make his hideous organism more prominent and obtrusive; the object of passion in order to stimulate the raging debility of exhausted sensuality, must be an adultress, a step-mother, or a sister; with a reference to the atrocious indecencies of Don Juan I shall not pollute my page.

Here we have the accusation of misanthropy and infliction of pain for its own sake as well as denial of any corrective intent. And with this accusation is coupled sheer vilification of the author and ambiguous reference to the "atrocious indecencies" of the poem. The complete absence of literary criticism in this review may be attributed, in part, to the extreme political prejudice of this conservative journal.

The remaining reviews of the first two cantos of *Don Juan* from which I quote are, in the main, more favorable than those already represented. The first is from the *New Monthly Magazine* for August 1, 1819, and is signed "W. C." The reviewer praises the excellences of the poem and condemns its lapses with an admirable restraint. There is in this review a moderation and a tolerance that are lacking in some of the foregoing reviews.

. . . . We lament to behold so much fervid genius, elegant literature, and knowledge of the world, united with a spirit of libertinism and infidelity, and employed to corrupt the senses . . . . We cannot read these passages without being touched by their exquisite beauty, and wishing that a poet so full of the true inspiration had devoted his powers to the cause of virtue. The fire of imagination in these brilliant pictures, and the melody of versification are worthy of Moore, or Byron, or Scott, or Campbell, or any other poet of the age . . . . we are reminded more of Lord Byron's style than that of any other living poet . . . .

. . . . But in *Don Juan*, although the unknown writer evinces powers as high and ardent as the noble poet, he does not so strongly and perpetually identify himself with his principal character. He destroys that allusion by passing at once with a surprising and unaccountable indifference, from images of pathos, beauty, and grandeur to ludicrous and burlesque similes and expressions . . . .

We have done justice to his genius. We have condemned its abuse, and we calmly appeal from his present practice to his hopes of celebrity. A certain degree of fleeting reputation may be acquired by ministering to the fashionable follies and corruptions of the age; but no British poet can obtain a universal and permanent fame, excepting by the devotion of his muse to the interests of truth and justice, and the delineation of examples conducive to social happiness and virtue.[9]

The critic commends the poem for its passages of exquisite beauty and true inspiration and avers that in fire of imagination and melody of versification it is worthy of Byron. He points out the resemblances to Byron's style: the heightening of spirit and facilitation of movement by the interlinking of stanzas; the identification of the poet with his principal characters; and the "burning intensity" and "utter absorption" of the poet's every sense in the scene and object he is describing. It is to be noted, too, that the critic observes that "the author" of *Don Juan* does not

[9] *"Don Juan.* I–II," in *New Monthly Magazine,* XII (August 1819), 75–78.

identify himself with his chief character as completely as Byron customarily does—thinking, very likely, of *Childe Harold*.

However, the reviewer finds the sudden plunges from pathos and beauty to the ludicrous and the burlesque "surprising and unaccountable" and, thus, un-Byronic.

The reviewer regrets the uniting of such "fervid genius" with the spirit of libertinism and infidelity. Even the title suggests that the poet selected the progress of a rake as an appropriate vehicle for licentious description. The refinement and the glowing fancy of the poem but serve to render its descriptions insidiously dangerous.

He concludes his review with an expression of his solicitude for the poet's hopes of celebrity and a warning that no British poet can obtain a universal and permanent fame by "ministering to the fashionable follies and corruptions of the age," but, rather, by devoting his muse to the "interests of truth and justice." The tolerance of this review, appearing as it does in the politically conservative *New Monthly Magazine*, is somewhat less surprising when it is noted that its contributor, "W. C.," may well have been an outsider whose views were not illustrative of the critical attitude of that journal.

The last of the reviews from which I quote is the most favorable. It appeared in *The Monthly Review* for July 1819. *Don Juan* is here characterized as a "singular and very superior poem."

. . . . We might almost imagine that the ambition had seized the author to please and to displease the world at the same time . . . . He has here exhibited that wonderful versatility of style and thought which appear almost incompatible within the scope of a single subject; and the familiar and the sentimental, the witty and the sublime, the sarcastic and the pathetic, the gloomy and the droll, are all touched with so happy an art, and mingled together with such a power of union, yet such a discrimination of style, that a perusal of the poem appears more like a pleasing and ludicrous dream, than the sober feeling of reality . . . .

We hope, however, that his readers have learnt to admire his genius without being in danger from its influence; and we must not be surprised if a poet *will* not always write to instruct as well as to please us. Still we must explicitly condemn and reprobate various passages and expressions in the poem, which we shall not insult the understanding, the taste, or the feeling of our readers by pointing out . . . .[10]

This reviewer acknowledges and condemns the demerits of the poem, but without severity and alarm. The poet's ready command over the "real energy" and even "sublimity" of poetry, asserts the reviewer, is illustrated by his account of the shipwreck in mid-ocean and the subsequent miseries of the survivors. This favorable review, it must be noted, appears in a liberal Whig journal, and it is, thus, open to the suspicion of political prejudice in Byron's favor.

About two years after the first two cantos of *Don Juan* appeared, the periodical reviewers were supplied with fresh fuel for their fires by the publication on August 8, 1821, of Cantos III, IV, and V.

Presenting the less favorable reviews first, I quote next from the review which appeared in *The British Critic* for September 1821:

. . . . The Poem before us is one of these hole and corner deposits; not only begotten but spawned in filth and darkness. Every accoucher of literature has refused his obstetric aid to the obscure and ditch-delivered foundling; and even its father, though he has unblushingly stamped upon it an image of himself which cannot be mistaken, forbears to give it the full title of avowed legitimacy . . . .

[10] *"Don Juan.* I–II," in *The Monthly Review,* LXXXIX (July 1819), 314–21. *The Monthly Review* was a liberal Whig journal. William Taylor and Thomas Holcroft were among the many noted contributors. Cf. Graham, *op. cit.,* pp. 210–11.

Of the story of these cantos we cannot be expected to present any detail. It consists of a few scenes closely imitated from Louvet and Laclos (and this does not surprise us, for vice after all is drearily monotonous,) done into rhymes . . . . Besides these there is a profusion of episodical matter, from which we collect that matrimony is still the thorn in his lordship's flesh; that though now approaching to the confines of middle age and (if we are not misinformed) inclining to *embonpoint*, he is still desirous to be thought a *beau garçon*, and well with the ladies . . . .[11]

Here we witness the degeneration of criticism into abuse, insult, and personal ridicule. Byron is deceived in claiming Pulci for his model; the occasional licentiousness of the Italian poet is the result of an "overflowing of a mind too sportive for control" rather than, as in Byron's case, "the slowly concocted venom of deliberate wickedness."

The chief idea which this reviewer gains from the three cantos is that "matrimony is still the thorn in his lordship's flesh." The sheer vituperation of this review may well be charged to the well-nigh hysterical pitch to which political as well as religious prejudice had risen. *The British Critic*, it must be remembered, was Tory in politics.

The next review is higher in tone. *The Imperial Magazine* acknowledges the poet's high talents but deplores their misuse.

Again has the voice of the mighty autocrat of British poets sounded from the spot of his voluntary ostracism to the shore of this, his native country; long have the admirers of the noble bard been expecting the future cantos of *Don Juan;* and long have the friends of religion and morality been fearing for what should come next in the exquisitely disgusting details of this unprofitable, yea iniquitous poem. At last it is before the public, and neither of the above parties will probably be much disappointed

[11] *"Don Juan.* III–IV–V," in *The British Critic*, XVI (September 1821), 252–55.

in the perusal of these three cantos . . . . Two things yet appear to be his Lordship's abomination . . . . marriage and society . . . . yet he has not only the *poetry of nobility* but the *nobility of poetry.*[12]

There is here a definite note of remonstrance with the "mighty autocrat of British poets" for his "voluntary ostracism" in a foreign land and his failure to make "his native country the soil of his productions." And there is a tacit appeal to the poet's innate nobility in the reviewer's assertion that there are few names in the peerage which he should more have honored than that of Byron had he chosen "piety and purity" as the "blandishments of his muse."

The reviewer insures the pleasing of both the admirers and censors of *Don Juan* in his diplomatic remark that neither the admirers of the noble bard, who have been anticipating the new cantos, nor the friends of religion and morality, who have been "fearing for what should come next," will "probably be much disappointed." The details of this "unprofitable" and "iniquitous" poem are "exquisitely disgusting" and must inevitably leave a "trace or taint on the heart" of him who reads them. This review is illustrative of some degree of emancipation from the critical phobias of the period. It almost approximates "literary" criticism.

The Monthly Review, whose review of the first two cantos of *Don Juan* was the most favorable of those from which I quoted, was still mild in its criticism of the new cantos but unenthusiastic and inclined to be bored.[13]

---

[12] "Lord Byron's *Don Juan,*" in *The Imperial Magazine,* III (1821), 945–47. *The Imperial Magazine* was first published in 1760 "by His Majesty's authority." Cf. Graham, *op. cit.,* p. 178.

[13] "*Don Juan.* III–IV–V," in *The Monthly Review,* XCV (August 1821), 418–20.

. . . . In plain terms, we conceived that we were not to behold any additional cantos of this poem; and the author of it now acknowledges that he was apprized of the prevailing sentiment against it. He does not, however, appear willing to yield to any such suggestion, farther than by a compromise: that is, he resolves to continue to write, but promises to write more circumspectly, though he should in that case write less wittily. . . . .

This "self-denying ordinance" has certainly been in part observed by the poet, but we shall not predict that his success in this respect will be deemed complete; . . . . but moreover, Lord Byron (whom we may still name as the author, though he here continues to write anonymously), now makes his narration much too narrative, and his excursions much too excursive; and he will scarcely induce his readers to be pleased with digressions that become tiresome, by admitting that he is conscious of his wandering habits, and cannot refrain from them. . . . . *Interest,* therefore, a primary consideration in these cases, is almost entirely sacrificed; and all the hold on its readers which the tale maintains is derived from occasional passages of beauty, and striking thoughts, without which no poem by Lord Byron can appear. . . . .

The whole employment of the poem, concludes the reviewer, has hitherto been, and apparently will continue to be, a "series of love-intrigues" and the "mere repetition of sensual attachment and 'casual fruition'." Here is a more favorable review. But the motivation of political prejudice can still be suspected, as the review appears in a liberal Whig journal.

Blackwood's Edinburgh Magazine for August 1821 contained a letter concerning the three new cantos of *Don Juan* addressed to "Christopher North" and signed "Harry Franklin."[14] The pervading spirit of the letter is urbane and tolerant, and it generously praises the beauties of the poem.

[14] "Letter to Christopher North," in *Blackwood's Edinburgh Magazine*, X (August 1821), 107–15.

As I know you have a confounded moral ill-will at Byron, and lately threw yourself into a devil of a passion at his racketing boy, Don Juan, I have determined, before you can get the three new Cantos, to put it out of your power, for a month at least, to say one uncivil word on the subject— . . . . In the first place, then, Christopher, I take leave to insist that these three cantos are like all Byron's poems, and by the way like everything else in this world, partly good and partly bad. In the particular descriptions they are not quite so naughty as their predecessors. . . . .

I have however given enough from the poem to convince you that Byron's powers are in no degree abated, and that there is some tendency to an improvement of manners . . . . [but as for moral tendency] it will be found as bad as ever . . . . —Lord Byron may have his faults,—you may have your own, my good friend, but there is some difference between constitutional errors, and evil intentions, and propensities,—it is harsh to ascribe to wicked motives what may be owing to the temptations of circumstances, or the headlong impulse of passion. Even the worst habits should be charitably considered, for they are often the result of the slow, but irresistible force of nature, over the artificial manners and discipline of society. . . . . Man towards his fellow-man should be at least compassionate, for he can be no judge of the instincts and the impulses of action, he can only see effects. . . . . In short, Christopher, look to thyself, and believe me truly yours,   HARRY FRANKLIN.

The gentleness and mild remonstrance of this delightful letter is in pronounced contrast to the hostility and denunciation of many of the preceding reviews. Among the beauties of the poem he praises the description of Haidée, the return of Lambro, the bacchanalian lyric, "The Isles of Greece," and the reverent "Ave Maria" lines.

But, alas, the reviewer laments, Byron's morals are as bad as ever. Only infants can be shown naked in company, but Byron strips both men and women before our eyes.

For this he is culpable and deserving of a drubbing, as well as for his slovenly verse-making.

And here "Harry Franklin" becomes the first reviewer to contradict the assertion of earlier critics that Byron's purpose in the poem is deliberate intent to corrupt morals. This reviewer insists that Byron is not chargeable with deliberate intent to corrupt and to leer at virtue and morality. Even the worst of his faults may be owing to the "temptations of circumstances" or the "headlong impulse of passion" rather than to "wicked motives" and evil propensities.

This review in a Tory journal is notable as an exception to the political bias of periodical criticism of the period.

The two leading journals of the day, *The Edinburgh Review* and *The Quarterly*, were still silent with regard to *Don Juan*. In August 1821 *The Edinburgh Magazine*, in a review of the three new cantos, deliberately asked why these two leading critical organs had allowed this poem to obtrude its immorality and irreligion "in every quarter of the United Kingdom" without their reprobation. In short, *The Edinburgh Magazine* challenged these journals to speak.[15]

Here is my Lord Byron, doubtless one of the most extraordinarily gifted intellectual men, again enacting the part of Don Juan again, and with impunity, poisoning the current of fine poetry, by the intermixture of ribaldry and blasphemy such as no man of pure taste can read a *second* time, and such as no woman of correct principles can read the *first*. Why is this ridiculous and disgusting farce to go on, unnoticed by the more powerful critical journals of the day? Where sleeps that well disciplined and master spirit, which once inflicted chastisement upon the aberrations of a muse which has since become bewitching from its

---

[15] *"Don Juan.* III–IV–V," in *The Edinburgh Magazine*, a New Series of the *Scots Magazine*, LXXXVIII (August 1821), 105–8. The journal was originally Jacobite in its sympathies, and consistently liberal. Cf. Graham, *op. cit.*, pp. 164–65 and 373.

modesty? Does the editor of another *quarterly* journal also sleep? Whence this soporific enchantment? What has benumbed the feelings, or hushed the indignation of the great champions in modern literature? . . . .

And as for the cantos recently published, we reserve a more close criticism on them for a future number. . . . .

. . . . We wish, we heartily wish, that the fine poetry, which almost redeems the third Canto (the least exceptionable on the ground of immorality) from reprobation, had not been mixed up with very much that is equally frivolous and foolish. . . . . Meanwhile, it may be as well for him to consider, that the public soon tire of *monstrosity,* both in morals and in literature.

It finds that the new cantos abound in grossness and personal abuse and are sadly wanting in the "vis poetica," whether of plot or execution; they are "barren of incident, but fruitful of digression." Byron's "religious creed" in stanza civ of Canto III is what one would expect from the "leader of banditti."

However, the reviewer allows, this "third Canto" has almost enough fine poetry to redeem it from reprobation. "The second stanza in this Canto is beautiful and almost original." And the heroic hymn is "one of the very finest things, of its kind, of modern poetry." He lauds its vigor of thought and expression, and "the fine classical feeling which pervades the whole."

This, again, is an exceptional review inasmuch as it is a condemnatory criticism in a liberal journal. However, it descends below the level of literary criticism and is motivated by religious prejudice.

The Edinburgh Review finally broke its silence in an article on "Lord Byron's *Tragedies*" by Francis Jeffrey which appeared in February 1822.[16] It is well to remem-

---

[16] "Lord Byron's *Tragedies,*" in *The Edinburgh Review,* XXXVI (February 1822), 446–52. The *Edinburgh* was the unofficial organ of the Whigs. Cf. Graham, *op. cit.,* pp. 233–34.

ber as one examines Jeffrey's strictures that they concern the entire five cantos of *Don Juan* which had appeared prior to his writing of this review.

Jeffrey wrote:

. . . . *We* are not bigots, nor rival poets. We have not been detractors from Lord Byron's fame, nor the friends of his detractors; and *we* tell him—far more in sorrow than in anger— that we verily believe the great body of the English nation—the religious, the moral, and the candid part of it—consider the tendency of his writings to be immoral and pernicious—and look upon his perseverance in that strain of composition with regret and reprehension. . . . .

. . . . We do not charge him with being either a disciple or an apostle of Satan; nor do we describe his poetry as a mere compound of blasphemy and obscenity. On the contrary we are inclined to believe that he wishes well to the happiness of mankind—and are glad to testify, that his poems abound with sentiments of great dignity and tenderness, as well as passages of infinite sublimity and beauty . . . .

The charge we bring against Lord B. in short is, that his writings have a tendency to destroy all belief in the reality of virtue— and to make all enthusiasm and constancy of affection ridiculous; and that this is effected, not merely by direct maxims and examples, of an imposing or seducing kind, but by the constant exhibition of the most profligate heartlessness in the persons of those who had been transiently represented as actuated by the purest and most exalted emotions—and in the lessons of that very teacher who had been, but a moment before, so beautifully pathetic in the expressions of the loftiest conceptions. . . . .

This is the charge which we bring against Lord Byron. We say that, under some strange misapprehension as to the truth, and the duty of proclaiming it, he has exerted all the powers of his powerful mind to convince his readers, both directly and indirectly, that all ennobling pursuits, and disinterested virtues, are mere deceits or illusions—hollow and despicable mockeries for the most part, and, at best, but laborious follies . . . .

. . . . We have already said, and we deliberately repeat, that we have no notion that Lord B. had any mischievous intentions in these publications—and readily acquit him of any wish to corrupt the morals, or impair the happiness of his readers. Such a wish, indeed, is in itself altogether inconceivable; but it is our duty, nevertheless, to say, that much of what he has published appears to us to have this tendency— . . . .

Thus spake the autocrat of British critics to the autocrat of British poets!

To round out Jeffrey's strictures: He avers that the public has been "clearly" and "constantly" just to Byron's genius and "signally indulgent" of his faults. Byron has accepted the praise but spurned the advice of his well-wishers and has only aggravated his offenses as he has grown in fame and influence. Byron would fain persuade himself that the censure which has been visited upon him since the appearance of *Don Juan* is owing not to any actual demerits of his own but to the jealousy of those he has supplanted and the party rancor of those he has offended. Not so, says Jeffrey—"The party that Lord Byron has offended bears no malice to Lords and Gentlemen." It is not merely the base and the bigoted who censure Byron. It is true that such have taken advantage of the prevailing anti-Byron sentiment to indulge in "silly nicknames" and "vulgar scurrility." Byron has, however, alienated his natural defenders.

Lord Byron, says Jeffrey, need fear no "priestlike cant or priestlike reviling" from the *Edinburgh*. His poems abound in passages of dignity and tenderness, and of "infinite sublimity and beauty." We reprehend his audacious speculation, his erroneous and indefensible assertions, his indecencies, seductive descriptions, and profligate representations. But in these respects he is not more guilty than Dryden, Prior, Fielding, or "other classical or pardoned writers." And the precedent of leniency might even have been followed with regard to his skepticism, misanthropy, and pessimism had not these been placed in juxtaposition to touching pictures of tenderness, generosity, and faith.

This brings Jeffrey to his major charge against Byron, namely, that his writings have a tendency "to destroy all belief in the reality of virtue" and "to make all enthusiasm and constancy of affection ridiculous" by constantly representing the coexistence of the most pure and exalted emotions and the most profligate heartlessness in the same person. Thus he confounds and confuses our notions of right and wrong and shakes to the foundations our confidence in virtue and our reliance on truth and fidelity. We are led by his seductive simulation of utter sincerity to follow him in his apparent exaltation of all good and sublime feelings, only to be suddenly plunged into "mockery of all things serious or sublime," and we are brought back at once to the "substantial doctrine of the work"—the nonexistence of constancy in women or honor in men, and the folly of expecting to meet with any such virtues, or of cultivating them, for an undeserving world. Were Byron's purpose the satirizing of hypocrisy in human professions and institutions, it would be a different matter. But Byron's sarcasms are aimed not at hypocrisy but at mankind.

Here we have, in this tolerant and just review, true *literary* criticism for the first time. And, although it appears in a Whig journal, its favorable tone is owing obviously not to political prejudice but rather to the critic's fairness.

In July 1822 *The Quarterly* followed the example of the *Edinburgh* and noticed *Don Juan* for the first time in a review of Byron's dramas.[17] *The Quarterly*, like the *Edinburgh*, did not devote a separate article to *Don Juan*

---

[17] "Lord Byron's *Dramas*," in *The Quarterly*, XXVII (July 1822), 476–77. *The Quarterly*, strong Tory champion, was founded to counteract the Whiggism of the *Edinburgh*.

but took notice of it in a review of Byron's dramas. Heber, the writer of this review, stated that the journal had remained silent from a "conflict of admiration and regret."

. . . . But it was from this very conflict of admiration and regret;—this recollection of former merits and sense of present degradation;—this reverence for talent and scorn of sophistry, that we remained silent . . . .

. . . . We knew not any severity of criticism which could reach the faults or purify the taste of *Don Juan*, and we trusted that its author would himself, ere long, discover, that if he continued to write such works as these, he would lose the power of producing anything better, and that his pride, at least, if not his principle, would recall him from the island of Acrasia.

The Quarterly, asserts Heber, was among the first and warmest eulogists of the earlier fruits of Byron's genius. But it is with keen regret that this journal has witnessed the systematic and increasing "prostitution" of Byron's genius to the expression of abhorrent feelings and opinions. It is for this very reason that this journal has remained silent, trusting that Byron would, of himself, eventually learn that "wickedness was not strength, nor impiety courage, nor licentiousness warm-heartedness, nor an aversion to his own country philosophy," and would, with maturity, become such a poet as "virgins might read, and Christians praise, and Englishmen take pride in."

In the strictures of this Tory review, one can trace the taint of the dominant critical prejudices of the day.

Throughout the year 1822 letters and notes and comments on Byron's *Don Juan* continued to appear in English magazines and newspapers, though there were no more separate reviews of consequence devoted entirely to the poem until additional cantos appeared in the following year. Between August 1821 and April 1822 *Blackwood's Edinburgh Magazine* seldom appeared without one or more letters of censure or defense of Byron contributed by readers of the journal. The following letter to Christopher North which appeared in February 1822 is typical:

I will not dwell on the demerits of Don Juan, which have been, perhaps, much exaggerated by the fastidious prudery of this age. . . . . At present, there is at least an affectation of superior sanctity,—an attempt to preserve the appearance of greater delicacy and decorum. . . . . It [Don Juan] might have escaped much of the censure which has fallen on its immoral tendency, which is certainly not beyond what might be extracted from the productions of poets by no means branded with the stamp of profligacy, had not the noble author shown himself on all occasions the armed champion of libertinism, and, as it were, boasted of some of the worst propensities of human nature. . . . . By giving his hero this name he is supposed to possess all the qualities originally imputed to him.[18]

Here we have the bold assertion that the demerits of Don Juan have been, perhaps, much exaggerated "by the fastidious prudery of this age" and by its "affectation of superior sanctity." This contributor also makes the true observation, which had escaped the critics thus far, that the poem might have escaped much of the censure with which it had been visited had not Byron's licentious and profligate actions corroborated the worst suspicions of his detractors and colored and influenced their criticisms. As we shall see, it was often the case that the critics of Byron were so occupied with Byron's actions that they could not look clearly at his poetry. Here we have a condemnation of the unliterary criticism of the day, a refreshing exception to the party rancor and hypocrisy of most of the reviews.

The following postscript appended to a letter to Christopher North which appeared in Blackwood's in April 1822 requires no comment:

[18] "Letter to Christopher North on Lord Byron's Dramas," in Blackwood's Edinburgh Magazine, XI (February 1822), 212–13.

P.S. Print this *sine demur*. But as you value the preservation of Maga from the bottomless gulph of Bathos, issue a decree, forbidding all contributors, whosoever or whate'er they may be, to discuss the merits or demerits of Lord Byron, for the space of nine calendar months from the date of this Number. Do, for novelty's sake, give us some respite.[19]

On July 15, 1823, Cantos VI, VII, and VIII of *Don Juan* appeared with a "Preface" by Lord Byron, dated "Pisa, July, 1822," in which, among other things, he vigorously answered the major objection which had been raised against the already published cantos of the poem. This charge of "immorality" he characterized briefly as *"Cant"*—the "crying sin of this double-dealing and false-speaking time of selfish spoilers." Byron also indulged in a fierce lampoon of Castlereagh. It is not impossible that this preface incensed the English even more than the new cantos themselves.

Blackwood's began the inevitable barrage of criticism with the epithet, "garbage!"[20]

Alas! that one so gifted . . . . should descend to the compo sition of heartless, heavy, dull, anti-British garbage, to be printed by the Cockneys, and puffed in the Examiner. . . . . But so it is. . . . .

Southey, Gifford, etc., have their faults—above all they have their affectations—but, Heaven preserve us! what a plunge it is from their *worst* to the *best* that even Lord Byron seems capable of giving us since his conjunction with these deluded drivellers of Cockaigne!

Here we have the new cantos denounced as "garbage" and "filth" and disparaged as "heartless," "heavy," "dull," and "monotonous." There are not twenty readable

---

[19] "To Christopher North," in *Blackwood's Edinburgh Magazine*, XI (April 1822), 465.

[20] "*Don Juan*. VI–VII–VIII," in *Blackwood's Edinburgh Magazine*, XIV (July 1823), 88–92.

stanzas among three hundred! Lord Byron has lost his ear "not only for the harmony of English verse, but for the very jingle of English rhymes." The result is an "unmusical drawl" abounding with "bad rhymes." In fact, the versification is so hopeless that certain stanzas can be truthfully dubbed not only "prose" but very "dull prose" to boot. And the reviewer prints three stanzas (VI, v; VII, xxi; VIII, xxxi) as prose to exemplify his assertion.

Byron, his incensed critic maintains, decries chastity, sneers at matrimony, curses wives, abuses monarchy, deprecates lawful government, and exalts Jacobinism. The most astounding part of this review is the writer's assertion that the *best* which Byron is able to offer in his *Don Juan* is far below the *worst* of Southey, Gifford, etc.

The reviewer does discover some half-dozen or so stanzas "not quite unworthy of the better days of Lord Byron." But he does not bother to tell us which they are. He exhorts Byron to "pull up" and make at least one more exertion "worthy of himself" and of the expectations of a reading public which has "unwillingly deserted" and would "most gladly return to him."

And, finally, the reviewer takes issue with those who insist that Byron is a "deliberately, resolvedly wicked man. I know him . . . . from report . . . . to be a kind friend, where his friendship is wanted. I cannot consent to despair of Lord Byron . . . ."

This is another Tory review illustrative of the operation of political partisanship in periodical criticism.

In the same month *The Literary Gazette* assailed the new cantos with the epithet "moral vomit."[21]

This *little* book purposes to be a continuation of Lord Byron's

---

[21] *"Don Juan.* VI, VII, VIII," in *The Literary Gazette*, July 19, 1823, pp. 451–53. *The Literary Gazette* had been founded in 1817. Its first two editors were William Jerdan and Samuel Phillips. Cf. Graham, *op. cit.*, p. 315.

often beautiful and thoroughly licentious poem. . . . . But either satiety has supervened from the too frequent dosing of the sensual Muse, or his Lordship, late of Pisa, has lost all his powers except those of over-grossness and indecency. We know that a common sense of propriety is called cant, and an ordinary feeling of taste, hypocrisy, by Lord Byron and his pitiable suite. . . . . as a moral vomit we shall leave it untouched between the author and a sickened public. . . . .

. . . . As a composition the poem is seldom above doggrel, with rhymes and divisions between every possible part of speech . . . .

With some asperity the reviewer hastens to assure Byron that what he characterizes as cant and hypocrisy are only a "common sense of propriety" and "an ordinary feeling of taste." The substance of Canto VI he denounces as "gloating brutality of a wretched debauchee" wallowing in the "sty of his own luxury" like a "drivelling dotard." Even the veriest profligate, he says, knows that the details of his vices "cannot gratify another by report." The descriptions in Canto VI are worthy of Rabelais "divested of wit." The most obscene allusions are unblushingly hazarded and defended on the authority of Voltaire, referring here to Byron's "Preface." The most sacred subjects are "sedulously sought" for profanation.

Among the few beauties of the poem the reviewer selects the description of the sleeping maidens in the harem. As for the Siege of Ismail, it is but an "indifferent paraphrase" of the account given in the *Histoire de la Nouvelle Russie*. The reviewer concludes his faint praise with the quoting of eight stanzas in which glory and war are "moralled." This review furnishes a striking example of the substitution of moral "cant" and prudery for the standards of critical judgment.

The British Magazine for August 1, 1823, deplored the direction of Byron's "unquestionable genius" into such unworthy channels as "this monstrous offence against decorum and honesty—this opprobrium never to be removed from a once bright reputation."[22]

. . . . Lord Byron, after having achieved a rapid and glorious fame, has, by the publication of three additional Cantos of *Don Juan,* not only disgusted every well-regulated mind, and afflicted all who respected him for his extraordinary talents, but has degraded his personal character lower than even his enemies (of whom he has many) could have wished to see it reduced. . . . . We know that we ought to censure him, and we do so, but we cannot help pitying him still more.

The reviewer for this journal does not deny Byron's "unquestionable" genius but laments its "gratuitous," "melancholy," and "despicable" prostitution. It is true that licentious poetry is nothing new, but Lord Byron cannot write even in this "unworthy style" more than ordinarily well. Furthermore, Byron's new cantos display laborious effort and lack of wit. Nearly the whole of the one hundred and twenty-six stanzas of Canto VI are so offensive, indecent, and so filled with "drunken, drivelling, old gentleman's after-dinner obscenity" that they will not bear description.

Like the reviewer of *The Literary Gazette,* he acknowledges the beauty of the seraglio scene. But the rest is characterized by "bad English, bad rhymes, bad taste, spurious wit, and glaring obscenity." This review offers another illustration of the perverse refusal to regard *Don Juan* from the standpoint of critical judgment.

The British Critic, in reviewing the new cantos in August 1823, begins in the same familiar vein of deprecation of the "perversion" of Byron's "splendid talents" but in-

---

[22] *"Don Juan. VI–VII–VIII,"* in *The British Magazine,* August 1, 1823, pp. 273–76. Graham (*op. cit.*) makes no mention of a magazine by this title at this time.

troduces a variation by remarking the change of theme in the new cantos from "seduction" to "radicalism."

> There was a time when the friends of literature and virtue mourned over the occasional perversion of Lord Byron's splendid talents, and anticipated the time when they might be unexceptionably employed. . . . . It is needless however to remark, that all expectations of this sort have long ago subsided in the minds of the more serious and thinking part of the community . . . .
>
> With the character of Juan, however, as hitherto exhibited, we have no more quarrel than with that of Tom Jones, or any other child of passion and impulse. Lord Byron knew very well that a character like the original Don Juan, or the heroes of Gil Blas and Peregrine Pickle . . . . would not have answered the purposes of seduction so well as the generous but ungovernable boy of seventeen, whom he has so artfully enveloped in a maze of temptation. Nor, indeed, do we think that these purposes are so systematically pursued in the present three cantos as in the first. . . . . It may not be foreign to the purpose to enquire why seduction has thus become a secondary object to proselytism [radicalism] in the mind of the noble lord . . . .[23]

Canto VI, says this reviewer, opens with "about thirty dull twaddling stanzas, spiced with an indecency or two" and an occasional touch of the "old starling song of himself." But, once past the disagreeable harem episode, Byron furnishes us with some dialogue which possesses a "great deal of character and terse humour." The reviewer refers to the dialogue between the Russian Marshal, Suwarrow, and the English adventurer, Johnson (VII, lviii–lxiii). He also praises the two thrilling stanzas with which Canto VII closes (lxxxvi–lxxxvii) as well as the opening stanzas of Canto VIII.

He goes on to say that Byron in these new cantos appears to have relegated "seduction" to a secondary place

[23] "*Don Juan.* VI–VII–VIII," in *The British Critic*, XX (August 1823), 178–87.

and to have "bestrode the broken-knee'd hobby-horse of Radicalism." In brief, Byron sought, at first, to attack with one sweep, "religion, national spirit, the honour of man, and the virtue of woman . . . ." But failing in this attempt to destroy the "bulwarks of society" and reduce mankind to a "naked" and "sylvan" state, Byron has chosen as his new purpose radical proselytism.

This Tory review illustrates one of the dominant fears of the period, the fear of political revolution. Its condemnation of Byron's radicalism crowds out any actual literary criticism.

The Gentleman's Magazine took little more notice of the new cantos than it had of the former ones. The new cantos it found inferior.[24]

The next portion of the poem his Lordship thought proper to publish [III, IV, V], was marked by the same immorality of purpose with very few of the attractive qualities for which the former part was so distinguished; but the Cantos which have given rise to these remarks [VI, VII, VIII] are incomparably the most abominable in spirit, and wretched in execution, of all the writings of the author. Many of the verses are merely disjointed prose, clipped into stanzas of eight lines each, without the least regard to their euphony . . . .

Here the reviewer assails Byron for his attack on Castlereagh in his "Preface" to Cantos VI, VII, and VIII. Then he continues:

The sixth Canto, without the wit which even to depraved minds can alone render such grossness attractive, is almost throughout, scandalously licentious and obscene, and fit only for the shelves of a brothel.

The reviewer then concludes his review with the quotation of a few of the "best stanzas." They are the descrip-

[24] "*Don Juan.* VI, VII, VIII, and IX, X, XI," in *The Gentleman's Magazine*, XCIII (September 1823), 250–52.

tion of the sleeping women in the seraglio (VII, lxiv–lxviii) and Juan's rescue of the Turkish child (VIII, xci–xcv).

In this review the tone of pharisaical virtue and moral bigotry is most conspicuous.

The next review of Cantos VI, VII, and VIII from which I quote appeared in two successive numbers of *The Portfolio*.[25]

Without stopping to inquire whether it be an act worthy of a great Poet to give his Pegasus the rein, and let him plunge headlong into every quagmire, we pass over the brief preface, in which the death of Lord Londonderry is treated somewhat irreverently, we think, considering the dreadful nature of the act, and proceed at once to the Poem.

In the midst of some keen, but unpolished wit, Lord Byron (for there cannot be a doubt that he is the writer) occasionally favours us with beautiful poetry. . . . .

Such are the three new cantos of *Don Juan*, which like their predecessors are liable to the same objections, and are equally sensible, witty, and keenly satirical; they will obtain the same applause or censure, according to the political or religious bias of those who promulgate their opinions. . . . .

This reviewer makes plain that his one quarrel with Lord Byron is his exertion of his "brilliant talents" to "throw blandishments over vicious passion." He disclaims any sympathy with those who rail against Byron because his political opinions are different from their own. And he is quite ready to make allowance for the "influence of passion on the minds of youthful poets"—one can expect them to disregard the "starched rules of antiquated formality." But there is a *"line of demarcation,* which the interests of society demand should never be violated.

---

[25] *"Don Juan.* VI–VII–VIII," in *The Portfolio*, I (Numbers xxi and xxii, 1823), 330–48. This magazine is not mentioned by Graham.

. . . . The end of all writing should be to inculcate morality . . . ."

It is to be noted that the reviewer remarks Byron's "considerable ability" in stripping "royalty of its tinsel." Furthermore, he admits that in these new cantos there is some "keen, but unpolished wit" and occasional "beautiful poetry."

But, for the most part, the three new cantos are "liable to the same objections" as their predecessors and are "equally sensible, witty, and keenly satirical." The worshipers of royalty will rail at the promulgation of democratic principles; the canting bigot will cry "blasphemy"; the sensualist will gloat over its descriptions; while the sensible man will sigh to find high talents prostituted to vice and immorality. And with what motive? "To enable misguided genius to show its versatility at the expense of all that is great and glorious in our imperfect nature!"

This is another of the rare reviews which succeeds in escaping almost entirely from the fetters of the dominant critical prejudices. It denounces the censure of *Don Juan* which springs from religious bigotry and disclaims any political bias, even daring to approve Byron's political liberalism.

The last review of Cantos VI, VII, and VIII from which I quote appeared in *The Edinburgh Magazine* in August 1823.[26] This journal was among the first to recognize and approve Byron's satiric purpose in *Don Juan.*

The review opens with a condemnation of Byron's "manufacture of furniture for the brothel."

. . . . it does not occur to us, that what would certainly be a vice in any other man, ought to be held as a virtue in Lord Byron. For example, "the manufacture of furniture for the

---

[26] "*Don Juan.* VI–VII–VIII," in *The Edinburgh Magazine,* a New Series of the *Scots Magazine,* XCII (August 1823), 190–99.

brothel," or the scoffing at and blaspheming the Christian religion, have never, so far as we have discovered, been regarded
by anybody as very conclusive proof of modesty deep-seated in
the heart, or of a great superabundance of inherent religion and
virtue. His Lordship, however, entertains a different opinion and
attempts to justify his own practice by two pithy sophisms of that
most witty and obscene of all blasphemers, Voltaire. . . . .

We do not mean to deny that hypocrisy is fair game, wherever
it appears, and that "cant religious, cant political, cant moral and
cant critical," deserve all the contempt which his Lordship has
poured upon them: but religion, politics, ethics, and criticism,
are not to be proscribed on this account: the "cant religious" is
not religion; the "cant political" is not public principle; the "cant
moral" is not virtue; the "cant critical" is not honest and im-
partial criticism. Why will not his Lordship distinguish a little?
Why does not he assail the abuse instead of the thing abused?
. . . .

. . . . In spite of all his faults, Byron has a noble sympathy
with liberty, and a just abhorrence of the leagued and crowned
oppressors of the earth, now occupied in filling up the measure
of their crimes against humanity, and in attempting to crush that
spirit which they want the skill to guide, as much as the power
ultimately to subdue, and which will one day break forth like an
overwhelming flood, uprooting their unhallowed thrones, and
sweeping away every fragment of despotism from the face of the
earth. . . . .

Byron, says the writer of the review, attempts to justify
his obscenity and religious blasphemy by "two pithy sophisms" of Voltaire. Is a woman to be held a hypocrite,
the writer asks with asperity, "because she will not talk
lewdly"? Is a man a hypocrite because he will not blas-
pheme his Maker and scoff at the truths of Christianity
or allow his understanding to be perverted by the shallow
sophistry of the French *philosophes?*

Byron has become the "Poet-Laureate of Lust" and to
the lowest purposes is devoting "his great and almost un-

rivalled genius." The first of the three new cantos (VI)
is "a piece of unredeemed and unrelieved sensuality and
indecency."

The reviewer does not, however, deny that "hypocrisy
is fair game," and that religious, political, moral, and
critical cant "deserve all the contempt which his Lordship
has poured upon them." But, urges the writer, why does
not Byron distinguish between true religion, politics, morals, and criticism and their imitations? The reason is that
Byron's purpose is not to assail the abuses of religion and
morality, "but to sap the very foundations of both . . . ."

After this reiteration of the serious charge which had
been flung at Byron by other critics, the reviewer turns to
a recounting of what is admirable in the poem. In Cantos
VII and VIII he finds "some very powerful descriptions,
and occasional passages of great beauty and strength."
Among these are the description of Suwaroff (VII, lv),
the bravery of the Tartar Khan and his sons (VIII, civ-
cxviii), and the "whole description of the assault of Ismail" (VIII), which might safely be placed "in compe-
tition with whatever is most powerful, vigorous, and striking, in English poetry."

But that which makes this review one of the most significant thus far is the critic's approval of Byron's satire of
tyranny and his applause of Byron's "noble sympathy
with liberty." He lauds Byron's "just abhorrence of the
leagued and crowned oppressors of the earth."

The unquestionable moral bigotry of a part of this
review is somewhat palliated by the reviewer's sincere
approval of Byron's satirical attack upon tyranny and his
sympathy with the cause of liberty. *The Edinburgh Magazine* was consistently liberal in politics.

On August 29, 1823, Cantos IX, X, and XI of *Don
Juan* were published. Among the most excessive of the
critical attacks upon these new cantos was the following

splenetic diatribe which appeared in *The Literary Gazette* on September 6, 1823.[27]

But now for the new cargo of *Don Juan,* in plain prose; not unlike itself. Lord Byron's name *now* commands no respect; and we know not that it would be any excuse for us that the low blackguard filth and indecency through which we travelled were the offscourings of a highly elevated station. When a nobleman adopts the style of a porter in which to utter the sentiments of a bagnio, as the King says in Hamlet, his "offence is *rank.*"

This review is one of the best examples of the scurrility and vilification which characterized much of the contemporary periodical criticism of *Don Juan.* The reviewer heaps derogatory adjective on adjective, epithet on epithet. The poem, which opens with a "miserable tirade against the Duke of Wellington and Waterloo," is "plain prose," "low blackguard filth." It has the "style of a porter," and the "sentiments of a bagnio"; it is pointless, "incoherent," "obscene," "vulgar," "unpoetical," "a metaphysical cloud of skepticism," and "destitute of anything like a comprehensive or correct idea." The new cantos constitute a "wretched mixture of everything wicked and silly"; they are a compound of "egotism," "slang," "dogrell," and they manifest "not one particle of talent." They would "debase a felon and disgrace a dungeon." In short, the poem is a "farrago of vice," "drivelling sensuality," "brutal insensibility," and "worthless poetry." The reviewer concludes his tirade with, "Never was there such an insult offered to the understandings and good feelings of mankind!"

The British Magazine, in the issue of September 1, 1823, bewailed Byron's literary decay.[28]

---

[27] *"Don Juan.* IX–X–XI," in *The Literary Gazette,* September 6, 1823, pp. 562–63.

[28] *"Don Juan.* IX–X–XI," in *The British Magazine,* September 1, 1823, pp. 296–99.

We mourn over Lord Byron's falling off from the high poetical destiny which once seemed to be assured to him as we should over the profligate apostacy of some dear friend, who had sacrificed to base lusts and sordid enjoyments all the hope and promise of his early fame. . . . .

We wish we were his next heir, or even his next of kin: it should go hard but that a writ *de lunatico inquirendo* should issue. In the meantime we leave him, praying for him, with the *Cloun* in Twelfth Night—"Thy wits the heavens restore! endeavour thyself to sleep, and leave thy vain bibble-babble."

The earlier cantos, the reviewer of *The British Magazine* complains, were bad enough, "the first in indecency, and the latter in dulness"; but these new cantos only unite these two qualities. The intrigue with Catherine is not even refined pruriency but the "gross and indecent" love of the "brothels" and its inspirations are of the "stews." He concludes his brief review with a charge against Byron of lunacy. Thus the review sinks to the utterly unliterary level of mere scurrility and personal abuse.

The Edinburgh Magazine, in a review[29] of the three new cantos in September 1823, asserted that Byron affects to become "the modern Juvenal" and admitted that Byron is a "keen and sometimes powerful satirist."

Ecce iterum Crispinus! in other words, Lord Byron, with three additional cantos of *Don Juan* at his back. . . . . These cantos are, in fact, nothing but measured prose, replete with bad puns, stale jests, small wit, indecency, and irreligion, and exhibiting none of those redeeming bursts of true poetical inspiration for which their predecessors were remarkable. From beginning to end, we could discern no trace of that lofty and fervid genius which produced Lambro's Song, and other passages of equal pith and moment. . . . . His Lordship plainly affects to become the modern Juvenal; and he is certainly a keen and sometimes a powerful satirist; but he will never equal the terseness and vigour

[29] *"Don Juan.* IX–X–XI," in *The Edinburgh Magazine,* a New Series of the *Scots Magazine,* XCII (September 1823), 357–60.

of the great original, however much he may surpass it in grossness and obscenity.

Here the reviewer quotes and praises the stanzas in which Byron tenders the olive branch to Jeffrey (X, xi–xix) and the *ubi sunt* stanzas (XI, lxxvi–lxxx).

Note here the reviewer's assertion that these new cantos possess *none* of the redeeming beauties for which the earlier cantos "were remarkable," also that he does give Byron credit for "keen and sometimes powerful" satire. Thus for the third time this liberal journal approves Byron's satirical intent.

The Gentleman's Magazine was even more laconic than usual in its notice of Cantos IX, X, and XI. In a review of Cantos VI to XI of *Don Juan*[30] its reviewer had this to say of the three latest cantos:

Though, blushing as we must to see a "Nobleman want manners," we cannot but be thankful that the hand which administered the poison has supplied the antidote. The three last cantos have effectively neutralised the mischief of their precursors. The halo of Genius has been extinguished for its perversion, in the nebulous dulness. . . . .

The British Critic for September 1823,[31] persevering in its "nauseous task" of reviewing *Don Juan,* finds that in this his latest "characteristic little specimen of the 'cheap and nasty' " Byron is grown "incurably dull."

. . . . Our present purpose is merely to enquire, and that in the shortest possible manner, how far he has in the present instance succeeded, or is likely to succeed, in serving the interests of the firm in which he has thought fit to become an active partner. . . . . The case is perfectly plain. Lord Byron has perceived too late that public opinion has connected him, more than he may

---

[30] "*Don Juan.* VI, VII, VIII, and IX, X, XI," in *The Gentleman's Magazine,* XCIII (September 1823), 252.

[31] "*Don Juan.* IX–X–XI," in *The British Critic,* XX (September 1823), 524–29.

approve, with the Riminists, or Cocknico-Carbonari, or whatever
name may rejoice the ears of the literary club which he has been
pleased to found at Pisa. As obvious must it have become to his
tact and observation, that these his chosen friends are scouted both
by Whig and Tory as a gang of despicable Pilgarlics, insensible
alike to English prejudices, English pursuits, English humour,
and the comforts of an English fireside. Alike coarse, fluttering,
and insignificant, their body collective has been roughly brushed
away, like a nauseous flesh fly, from the front of Whiggism on
which it crawled for awhile, and not even Lord Byron himself
has escaped a portion of the disgrace. The temperate, keen, and
gentlemanlike strictures, attributed to Mr. Jeffrey, representing
as they naturally do, the opinion of his party, on the conduct and
writings of Lord Byron, have been the death-blow to his Lordship's self-love. . . . .

How are the mighty fallen! We can hardly suppose that the
author of *Childe Harold* and *Sardanapalus* has grown incurably
dull. . . . .

Byron, the reviewer of *The British Critic* alleges, has
outraged the "common decency and common feeling" and
materially diminished his literary reputation by his *Don
Juan*. The reviewer lauds Jeffrey's "temperate, keen, and
gentlemanlike strictures . . . . on the conduct and writings
of Lord Byron,"[32] and asserts that Byron, "at a loss how
to vent his mortified feelings," starts from his "fawning
posture at the feet of Mr. Jeffrey" to "fly with the undis-
tinguishable fury of a mad dog at every other person and
thing which can command the respect, claim the forbear-
ance, or gratify the predilections of Englishmen." From
the King and the Duke of Wellington to the humblest
individual of the empire, "nothing escapes him."

This Tory review furnishes one of the clearest illustrations of the prevalent unliterary criticism motivated by
party rancor and fear of political liberalism.

[32] *The Edinburgh Review*, XXXVI (February 1822), 446–52.

In September 1823 *Blackwood's* printed a letter[33] to
Christopher North in which the writer implores North to
"abuse Wickedness, but acknowledge Wit" and exhorts
him to distinguish between "moral tendency" and "intellectual power."

Dear North,—I have a great respect both for old Tickler and
yourself, but now and then you both disquiet me with little occasional bits of lapses into the crying sin of the age—*humbug!*
What could possess him to write, and you to publish, that absurd
critique—if indeed it be worthy of any such name—upon the
penult batch of *Don Juan?* The ancient scribe must have read
those cantos when he was cropsick, and had snapped his fiddle
string. You must never have read them at all.

. . . . If you mention a book at all, say what it really is.
Blame *Don Juan;* blame *Faublas;* blame *Candide;* but blame
them for what really is deserving of blame. Stick to your own
good old rule—abuse Wickedness, but acknowledge Wit . . . .

I maintain, and always have maintained, that *Don Juan* is,
without exception, the first of Lord Byron's works. It is by far
the most original in point of *conception.* It is decidedly original
in point of *tone.* . . . . It contains the finest specimens of
serious poetry he has ever written; and it contains the finest
specimens of ludicrous poetry that our age has witnessed. . . . .
Don Juan, say the canting world what it will, is destined to
hold a permanent rank in the literature of our country. It will
always be referred to as furnishing the most powerful picture
of that vein of thought, (no matter how false and bad,) which
distinguishes *a great portion of the thinking people of our time.*
. . . .

And after all, say the worst of *Don Juan,* that can with fairness be said of it, what does the thing amount to? Is it *more*
obscene than Tom Jones? Is it *more* blasphemous than Voltaire's
novels? In point of fact, it is not within fifty miles of either of

---

[33] "Odoherty on *Don Juan,* Cantos IX, X, and XI," in *Blackwood's
Edinburgh Magazine,* XIV (September 1823), 282–93. "Odoherty"
was William Maginn, later one of the founders of *Fraser's Magazine.*
Cf. Graham, *op. cit.,* p. 279.

them: and as to the obscenity, there is more of that in the pious Richardson's pious Pamela, than in all the novels and poems that have been written since. . . . . Is he no longer a great author? Has his genius deserted him along with his prudence? Is his Hippocrene lazy as well as impure? Has he ceased, in other words, to be Byron, or is he only Byron playing mad tricks?

The latter is my opinion, and I propose to convince you, in case you are not already of the same mind, by quoting a few passages from the other three cantos that have just appeared—and which I humbly conceive to be the very best, in so far as talent is concerned, of all that have yet come forth. . . . .

The passages which he then quotes are the stanzas descriptive of Juan's arrival at the court of Catherine (IX, xlii ff.) and her amour with him (IX, lxvii ff.); the satire of Catherine scattered through Cantos IX and X; Donna Inez's hypocrisy (X, xxxi ff.); the rapid sketch of Juan's journey from Russia to England (X, lviii–lxv); the "exquisitely good" Shooter's Hill episode (XI, viii–xx); and the *ubi sunt* stanzas (XI, lxxvi–lxxx).

Finally, the writer urges North to publish these stanzas in order that they may be seen by "your readers" separated and distinct from the "beastliness" and "gross," "outrageous," "abominable filth" in the midst of which they occur in the original, and in order that the world may see that North still distinguishes between *moral tendency* and *intellectual power*. This review, appearing in a Tory journal, is one of the few examples of veritable literary criticism of *Don Juan* produced in Byron's day.

Cantos XII, XIII, and XIV of *Don Juan* appeared on December 17, 1823. In the same month *The British Critic* reviewed the new cantos, calling them "a dry fatiguing desert of cynical twaddle."[34]

"If I be not ashamed of my soldiers," says Falstaff, "I am a

[34] "*Don Juan*. XII–XIII–XIV," in *The British Critic*, XX (December 1823), 662–66.

soused gurnet." It appears pretty plainly, in spite of all Lord Byron's bravados, that the repeated sousings he has received from different quarters, and the diminution of his literary fame, as admitted even by himself in the present Cantos, and in former passages of *Don Juan,* have operated in disgusting *him* also with his ragged regiment of ex-English associates, and inspired him with the intention of "purging and living cleanly."

The reviewer for *The British Critic* finds the new cantos less offensive than their predecessors and duller. One of the rebuffs he refers to was the banishment of *Don Juan* from Murray's "polite sanctum" to the "two-penny book-stall." Byron, he believes, is on his good behavior in these cantos for he is "neither obtrusively indecent, pointedly blasphemous, nor scurrilously abusive." From force of habit he still continues to indulge in sarcasms about English women, the King, Shakespeare, and Wellington, "but in a more feeble and civil manner." As for the execution of the new cantos, he has still failed to recapture the "easy bantering tone of profligacy" characteristic of *Beppo.* And especially worthy of note is the reviewer's statement that Byron's hero has "sunk from the Don Juan of Molière, into the 'Giovanni in London' of the minor theatres. . . . ."

This politically biased Tory review repeats the strictures of earlier *British Critic* reviews of *Don Juan,* but with a noticeable diminution of asperity. Apparently the reviewer is unaware of the increasing radical indoctrination of the later cantos.

The opinion of *The Literary Gazette* for December 6, 1823, coincides with that of *The British Critic* in adjudging the three latest cantos of *Don Juan* less offensive than the earlier cantos. But here the attitudes of the two journals markedly diverge, for *The Literary Gazette* finds[35] that the new cantos "certainly exhibit a knowledge of life

[35] *"Don Juan.* XII, XIII, XIV," in *The Literary Gazette,* December 6, 1823, pp. 771–73.

and nature, and are written in a sportive satirical vein which renders them very entertaining."

Ambling, sometimes hobbling carelessly along, we have here three other Cantos of the everlasting *Don Juan;* but three Cantos which, if they do not display the same genius with the earliest of their predecessors, are not liable to the same reproach with either those, the best, or their later successors, the worst; and certainly exhibit a knowledge of life and nature, and are written in a sportive satirical vein which renders them very entertaining. . . . .

Juan being in England, it was to be expected that the author would indulge himself in drawing pictures of English manners; and he has fortunately adopted for his purpose a series of subjects in the top ranks of society. That, so far as he has gone, we observe nothing exceedingly great or virtuous we will not condemn as a fault: Hogarth's Love a la Mode, Marriage a la Mode, etc. etc. are not blamed on account of their almost solely exposing what is mean and vicious. On the poet's canvas marriage is a constant butt, and his shafts never fail to be aimed in that direction. . . . .

Here the reviewer praises the description of "Norman Abbey" and expresses his opinion that the house-guests "are from life." He then continues:

On suicide as on marriage and its mishaps, the poet is more striking than correct. Of sympathy and love we have more able touches. . . . .

The "trifling badinage" of these three cantos, thinks the reviewer for *The Literary Gazette,* while not comparable with "the higher efforts of Lord Byron," is entertaining and amusing. There are many "pretty passages" among much "ruins" and "rubbish," and the whole is a blend of "playfulness with acute observation" which suggests the school of Democritus.

The reviewer does not condemn Byron because he does not emphasize the "great or virtuous" in his pictures of English manners. He reminds the critics of Byron that

Hogarth's pictures are not blamed for their exposition of what is "mean and vicious."

However, with respect to the satire of marriage, Byron does give us "too much of one thing." The pervading spirit of the three cantos is "anti-matrimonial soreness."

But, with all allowance being made for his faults, Byron does give us "able touches" of sympathy and love as well as descriptive passages of power such as the stanzas on "Norman Abbey" (XIII, lv–lxvii). In fact, the whole is "a very amusing Beppoish effusion" displaying Byron's talents for "raillery and jest."

This journal, with no political irons in the fire, presents *Don Juan* in a somewhat more favorable light. Furthermore, the comparison with Hogarth indicates the critic's increasing emancipation from the moral bigotry of contemporary periodical criticism.

Cantos XII, XIII, and XIV were reviewed together with Cantos IX, X, and XI[36] in *Knights Quarterly Magazine* in December 1823. According to this review:

That Lord Byron is *now "less* than archangel *ruined,"* we may honestly affirm; and we refer to the six last cantos of *Don Juan* for the proof. . . . . Assuming his own character, and speaking in his own person, he is plunging deeper and deeper in the mire of his profaneness; and though we cannot sully our pages with a single passage of the abominable outrages upon decency which the latter cantos of *Don Juan* contain, we must openly say . . . . that Lord Byron must cease to be reckoned as the compeer of a Scott, a Wordsworth, or a Coleridge; but must

---

[36] Although these cantos are not specifically named in this review, it is evident that Cantos IX to XIV are the ones under consideration both from the contents of the review and from the words "we refer to the six last cantos of *Don Juan.*" The "six last cantos" at the time when this review was written were Cantos IX to XIV. The review appeared in *Knights Quarterly Magazine*, I (December 1823), 343–48. This magazine, which lived about one year, was edited by Charles Knight. Cf. Graham, *op. cit.*, p. 288.

be looked upon as the imitator and the rival of a Rochester, a Cleveland, or a Wilkes. . . . .

But we have spoken warmly of Lord Byron's vices, because they are evidently not transient aberrations, but crimes upon principle. . . . .

This reviewer can think of nothing too base with which to charge Byron. The greatest of his sins is "his outrageous contempt" of "awful and mysterious subjects." The writer refuses to "sully" his pages with a single passage of the "abominable outrages upon decency" with which the latter cantos are polluted.

In short, as a poet Lord Byron is *"extinct."* And again we hear echoed that most damning of all the charges brought against Byron: his "vices" are "crimes upon principle." He has determined to be the poet of *"the mob"*; and he mistakenly supposes that the winning of this large and important portion of society requires abuse of authority, contempt of national creed, and vulgarity and obscenity in its most "obtrusive, daring, and unmitigated" form.

In this review literary criticism is virtually extinct and the strictures appear to be motivated by religious bigotry, moral hypocrisy, and fear of political defection.

Cantos XV and XVI were published on March 26, 1824, and on April 3 appeared the last review of *Don Juan* of any length or consequence prior to Byron's death. This review,[37] which appeared in *The Literary Gazette*, is assuredly one of the most typical of what Byron called the "canting reviews" of his poem. A part of it reads:

Lord Byron's name is not affixed to this continuation of *Don Juan*; and it is so destitute of the least glimmering of talent, so wretched a piece of stuff altogether, that we are inclined to believe it the work of some imitator,—inferior in his best efforts to even the worst of the genuine bad Cantos which have preceded. If it

[37] *"Don Juan*. XV–XVI," in *The Literary Gazette*, April 3, 1824, pp. 212–13.

be really Lord Byron's, it is a sad proof of his very mistaken opinion, that whatever nonsense he may think proper to scribble is worthy of being read. But we cannot believe it to be his. . . . . It opens thus . . . . [Here the reviewer quotes the first ten stanzas of Canto XV, putting them in prose form.]

Vanity, trite reflections upon marriage, his Lady, himself,— themes of which everyone is sick, except the writer,—make up this contemptible publication; in which the versification is worthy of the sense,—if we may prostitute both words, for miserable doggrel and empty nothings . . . . [Here he quotes the stanza about Christianity (XV, xviii) and calls it "flings" at Christianity.]

Instead of the tomohawk of Byron, it looks like the piddling scratches of Leigh Hunt's pin—a doughty diatribe of a perishing Sunday Newspaper . . . .

We have sedulously sought in this publication for a passage or two which we could cite as doing credit to a writer of any celebrity; and in the following our readers will find every line that we could select with that view, and to do whatever justice was possible to the author . . . . [Here the reviewer quotes XV, xcix, XVI, viii–xi, and the ballad which Adeline sings (XVI, following stanza xl).]

At this rate, the work bids fair to be interminable, as it has been pernicious and contemptible.

This review, "destitute" as it is of "the least glimmering" of literary criticism (to employ against him some of the reviewer's own words), is one of the last and most typical examples of the unliterary criticism of *Don Juan*.

The latest review of Cantos XV and XVI prior to Byron's death was that of *The Monthly Review* in April 1824. I shall not quote this very brief notice,[38] as it consists merely of a few perfunctory statements about the subject matter of the cantos. The only criticism it con-

---

[38] *"Don Juan.* XV–XVI," in *The Monthly Review*, CIII (April 1824), 434. This is the last on E. H. Coleridge's list of contemporary reviews of *Don Juan*. See the Coleridge edition of Byron's poems, vi, xx.

tains occurs in the first sentence: "Little progress of the story is made in these additional cantos of this interminable poem." This desultory review appeared in the pages of a liberal Whig journal.

A summary of this survey of *Don Juan* reviews in contemporary periodicals is now in order. In the following list, containing seventeen reviews not indicated by Coleridge,[39] and not pretending to be exhaustive, a star marks each item not in Coleridge's list and a dagger marks each item not strictly a review of *Don Juan* since the references to *Don Juan* which it contains are incidental. Of the latter the first is a review of Byron's *Mazeppa* in the *Eclectic*, the second and third are reviews of Byron's dramas by Jeffrey and Heber in *The Edinburgh Review* and *The Quarterly*, respectively, and the fourth is a letter entitled "Letter to Christopher North on Lord Byron's *Dramas*" in *Blackwood's Edinburgh Magazine*.

Cantos I–II

Blackwood's Edinburgh Magazine, V (August 1819), 512–18.

The British Critic, XII (August 1819), 196–204.

The Monthly Review, LXXXIX (July 1819), 314–21.

**The Gentleman's Magazine*, LXXXIX (August 1819), 152.

New Monthly Magazine, XII (August 1819), 75–78.

**New Monthly Magazine*, November 1819, p. 381.

*†*The Eclectic Review*, XII (August 1819), 147–56.

Cantos III–IV–V

The British Critic, XVI (September 1821), 252–55.

**The Imperial Magazine*, III (1821), 945–47.

The Monthly Review, XCV (August 1821), 418–20.

[39] Ernest Hartley Coleridge, *The Works of Lord Byron: Poetry*, VI, xx.

Blackwood's Edinburgh Magazine, X (August 1821), 107–15.
**The Edinburgh Magazine*, LXXXVIII (August 1821), 105–8.
†*The Edinburgh Review*, XXXVI (February 1822), 446–52.
†*The Quarterly*, XXVII (July 1822), 476–77.
*†*Blackwood's Edinburgh Magazine*, XI (February 1822), 212–13.

Cantos VI–VII–VIII

Blackwood's Edinburgh Magazine, XIV (July 1823), 88–92.
The Literary Gazette, July 19, 1823, pp. 451–53.
**The British Magazine*, August 1, 1823, pp. 273–76.
**The British Critic*, XX (August 1823), 178–87.
**The Gentleman's Magazine*, XCIII (September 1823), 250–52.
**The Edinburgh Magazine*, XCII (August 1823), 190–99.
*The Portfolio, I (Numbers xxi and xxii, 1823), 330–48.

Cantos IX–X–XI

The Literary Gazette, September 6, 1823, pp. 562–63.
**The British Magazine*, September 1, 1823, pp. 296–99.
**The Edinburgh Magazine*, XCII (September 1823), 357–60.
**The British Critic*, XX (September 1823), 524–29.
**Blackwood's Edinburgh Magazine*, XIV (September 1823), 282–93.

Cantos XII–XIII–XIV

**The British Critic*, XX (December 1823), 662–66.
The Literary Gazette, December 6, 1823, pp. 771–73.
**Knights Quarterly Magazine*, I (December 1823), 343–48.

CANTOS XV–XVI

The Literary Gazette, April 3, 1824, pp. 212–13.
The Monthly Review, CIII (April 1824), 434.

II

AN APPRAISAL OF THE REVIEWS

The foregoing examination of the contemporary periodical reviews of *Don Juan* has revealed much censure
and some praise. The censure runs the gamut from mild
disapproval to scurrilous abuse and presents all degrees
of indignation, objurgation, and condemnation. The
praise concerns chiefly specific brief passages but does
include Byron's basically liberal attitude. The adverse
criticism of *Don Juan* and of Byron—for all distinction
between the poem and its author is ignored in the contemporary reviews—may be resolved into the major
charges of: immorality; irreligion; prostitution of genius;
deliberate intent to corrupt; lack of poetic value; contempt
for social institutions; satire without corrective intent; and
revolutionary indoctrination. The favorable criticism com-
prises emphasis upon: the high poetic value of the work;
the author's lack of deliberate intent to corrupt; its serio-
comic style; and Byron's serious and constructive satiric
purpose.

Twenty-one, or two-thirds, of the thirty-two reviews of
Don Juan listed above are preponderantly, if not wholly,
adverse. It would appear, from the close correlation
between the nature of the review and the politics of the
periodical in which it was published, that the adverse criticism was motivated primarily by party bias, alarm over
political and religious defection, and exaggerated moral
prudery, rather than by conscientious application of standards of true literary judgment.

The remaining one-third of the reviews may, with certain reservations already noted, be classed as favorable in the main. These eleven reviews range from rather grudging approval or moderate praise, in the majority of instances, to the only two examples of bona fide literary criticism which the pages of contemporary periodical criticism of *Don Juan* have to offer. These two reviews, one by Francis Jeffrey in a Whig journal and the other by William Maginn in a Tory journal, stand out like oases in a sterile desert of critical prejudice. The tolerance, candor, and balanced judgment of these, reflecting neither excessive censure nor praise, are in marked contrast to the well-nigh hysterical virulence of the typical contemporary published estimate of *Don Juan*. Although, as has been noted, even the favorable reviews are not entirely free of the suspicion of political bias, these two reviews of Jeffrey and Maginn seem to exemplify true literary criticism, a rarity among the periodical reviews of *Don Juan*.

Taking up the adverse criticism, let us first examine the charge of immorality, with its two phases, tendency to relax morals and deliberate intent to corrupt. I share the opinion of Francis Jeffrey, expressed in his review in *The Edinburgh Review* in February 1822, that Byron was not a "resolvedly wicked" man and that he was not guilty in *Don Juan* of deliberate intent to corrupt. My reasons for this conclusion are that Byron expressly denies any evil intent, that there is no support for the accusation of wickedness in any of the autobiographical and biographical materials of Byron which I have examined, and that there is no evidence in *Don Juan* of deliberate intent on Byron's part to corrupt morals. It is true, as Jeffrey admitted, that there is much in *Don Juan* that is morally relaxing in tendency, as far as its effect upon immature minds is concerned. As Hugh Walker has said, "There is much in *Don Juan* which it would be sublime simplicity to believe to be there for the purpose of reformation";[40] witness the passages scattered throughout the poem where Byron seems to relish the voluptuousness he describes.[41] There is licentious description that is apparently indulged in for its own sake. It may readily be granted that such poetry can exert a morally relaxing influence upon youthful and immature minds. But this is not to admit the justification of such detractions as were made by the majority of the contemporary reviewers of the poem. The following are entirely unwarranted: "gross," "grovelling," "bestial," and "degrading debauchery"; "filth"; "hole and corner deposit"; "nastiness"; "loathsome and raging sensuality." It is no wonder that the reviewers "refused to exemplify" such "obscenities" with quotations from the poem; to do so was impossible, for they do not exist. Byron was right in asserting that *Don Juan* was as moral as the works of Fielding, Smollett, Ariosto, and others.

And as for the morality of the poem in the larger sense—even if it is not, as Byron insisted, "the most moral of poems"[42]—it is profoundly moral in the true sense of being a social satire, a satire of the most flagrant abuses of Byron's day, as will be demonstrated in the subsequent section of this work.

Next, as to the charge of irreligion. Are the accusations of impiety, blasphemy, infidelity, profanation of sacred subjects, and contempt for Christianity valid?

Byron's first serious reference in *Don Juan* to things religious is in Canto II, stanza clxv, where he speaks of the English preachers, Barrow, South, Tillotson, and Blair,

---

[40] Hugh Walker, *English Satire and Satirists* (New York, 1925), p. 276.

[41] For instance: I, clxv–clxx; VI, lxx–lxxv; IX, liv–lvi and lxvii–lxxii; XVI, cxxii–cxxiii.

[42] Prothero, *op. cit.*, IV, 279. (To John Murray. Venice, February 1, 1819.)

as "the highest reachers of eloquence in piety and prose"
and states that he is in the habit of reading them every
week. The next of these allusions to religion is in the
beautiful "Ave Maria" stanzas in Canto III, stanzas cii–
civ. Here we have genuine reverence and sincere religious
feeling.

> Ave Maria! blessed be the hour!
>   The time, the clime, the spot, where I so oft
> Have felt that moment in its fullest power
>   Sink o'er the earth so beautiful and soft,
>
> . . . .
>
> Ave Maria! 'tis the hour of prayer!
>   Ave Maria! 'tis the hour of love!
> Ave Maria! may our spirits dare
>   Look up to thine and to thy Son's above!
>
> . . . .
>
> My altars are the mountains and the ocean,
> Earth, air, stars,—all that springs from the great Whole,
> Who hath produced, and will receive the soul.

The devout pantheism in the concluding lines of the
last stanza savors less of irreligion than of its opposite.

In the famous description of Norman Abbey in Canto
XIII is a stanza (lxi) in which Byron again alludes rever-
ently to the Virgin:

> But in a higher niche, alone, but crown'd,
>   The Virgin-Mother of the God-born Child,
> With her Son in her blessed arms, look'd round;
>   Spared by some chance when all beside was spoil'd;
> She made the earth below seem holy ground.
>   This may be superstition, weak or wild,
> But even the faintest relics of a shrine
> Of any worship wake some thoughts divine.

And in Canto XV, stanza xviii, occur Byron's references
to Christ which a reviewer of *The Literary Gazette*, ob-
tusely enough, called "flings at Christianity":

> And thou, Diviner still,
> Whose lot it is by man to be mistaken,
> And thy pure creed made sanction of all ill?
> Redeeming worlds to be by bigots shaken,
> How was thy toil rewarded?

Here Byron sounds a very modern note in condemning historical Christianity in contrast to Christ's "pure creed." To this stanza Byron appended this note:

> As it is necessary in these times to avoid ambiguity, I say that I mean, by "Diviner still," CHRIST. If ever God was man— or man God—he was *both*. I never arraigned his creed, but the use, or abuse—made of it.[43]

At the opening of Canto XVI, in a digression concerning belief in supernatural visitations, stanza vi, Byron states:

> I do not speak profanely, to recall
> Those holier mysteries which the wise and just
> Receive as gospel, and which grow more rooted,
> As all truths must, the more they are disputed.

These are the sum of Byron's serious references to things religious in *Don Juan*. The adjectives "impious," "blasphemous," and "profane" are not applicable to any of them.

And now for his ironical and satirical allusions to religion and things religious. The first is a jocular allusion to the Virgin Mary in Canto I, stanzas lxxv and lxxvi. Julia, trying to decide between her love for the youthful Juan and fidelity to her husband,

> Prayed the Virgin Mary for her grace,
> As being the best judge of a lady's case.

[43] Byron's *Poetical Works* (Oxford University Press, 1928), pp. 901–2.

The next (I, lxxxiii) is a bit of irony about the consolations of conscience:

> A quiet conscience makes one so serene!
> Christians have burnt each other, quite persuaded
> That all the Apostles would have done as they did.

In stanza clxviii in the same canto, Byron jokes about David and Bathsheba, innocuously enough.

In the description of the shipwreck in Canto II, stanza xxxiv, Byron indulges in this diverting sally:

> There's nought, no doubt, so much the spirit calms
> As rum and true religion . . . .

A little farther on (II, lv) Byron pokes fun at the Catholic mass for souls in purgatory:

> When over Catholics the ocean rolls,
>   They must wait several weeks before a mass
> Takes off one peck of purgatorial coals,
>   Because, till people know what's come to pass,
> They won't lay out their money on the dead—
> It costs three francs for every mass that's said.

And, again, Byron tells us (II, cxlix) that Juan was so fond of women

>   . . . . that even when he pray'd
> He turn'd from grisly saints, and martyrs hairy,
> To the sweet portraits of the Virgin Mary.

The following is an instance (V, xxviii) of Byron's frequent use of the adjective "Christian" in a disparaging sense to emphasize the hollowness and hypocrisy of much that goes by that name:

> They haggled, wrangled, swore, too—so they did!
>   As though they were in a mere Christian fair,
> Cheapening an ox, an ass, a lamb, or kid . . . .

The avarice of the clergy is the subject of a jibe in Canto VII where (lxiv) he speaks of the preacher "who

nobly spurned all earthly goods save tithes." He again
satirizes the modern preacher (VII, vi):

> Ecclesiastes said, "that all is vanity"—
> Most modern preachers say the same, or show it
> By their examples of true Christianity:

And in the Amundeville house party (XIII, lxxxvii) is

> . . . . the Reverend Rodomont Precisian,
> Who did not hate so much the sin as sinner.

The next passage (XI, v–vi) is Byron's satire of "sick-
bed orthodoxy," which the horrified reviewers denounced
as "blasphemous":

> The truth is, I've grown lately rather phthisical:
>   I don't know what the reason is—the air
> Perhaps; but as I suffer from the shocks
>   Of illness,[44] I grow much more orthodox.
>
> The first attack at once proved the Divinity
>   (But *that* I never doubted, nor the Devil);
> The next, the Virgin's mystical virginity;
>   The third, the usual Origin of Evil;
> The fourth at once established the whole Trinity
>   On so uncontrovertible a level,
> That I devoutly wish'd the three were four
> On purpose to believe so much the more.

False piety comes in for a jibe in Canto V, stanza vi;
and hypocrisy in prayer receives a thrust in stanza xxiii of
Canto VI. Finally, in Canto X, stanza xxxiv, Byron strikes
the keynote of his satire of religious hypocrisy in his use
of the word "parson" in these lines:

---

[44] Byron actually was ill when he wrote these stanzas, as is shown
by his statement in a letter to Murray in which he says that he has
finished a "5th" (the 10th) canto and begun the eleventh. See Prothero, *op. cit.*, VI, 121. (To John Murray. October 9, 1822.)

> Oh for a *forty-parson power* to chant
> Thy praise, Hypocrisy! Oh for a hymn
> Loud as the virtues thou dost loudly vaunt,
> Not practise!

Such allusions to religion and things religious elicited the harsh words, "blasphemy," "impiety," "infidelity"! There is, to be sure, levity with regard to things religious. But Byron's intent is clear. He jokes about the superficialities of religion and he satirizes religious hypocrisy.

The next major charge preferred against Byron and his *Don Juan* is that in the poem Byron prostituted his "high," "extraordinary," and "unquestionable" genius to low purposes. Let us see if there is any justification for alleging that Byron's purpose in *Don Juan* is a low one. As I have already indicated, Byron's dominant purpose throughout the entire poem is satirical. Byron's original motive was, as he expressed it, "To be a little quietly facetious about everything."[45] While the first five cantos are playfully ironic in spirit, the emphasis is primarily upon incident. But with the third group of cantos (VI, VII, and VIII), the emphasis shifts to serious satire. It becomes "a Satire on *abuses* of the present states of Society"[46] and it is, as will appear in the subsequent section, a social satire of serious intent and of positive significance.

Closely related to the charge of prostitution of high talents, if not actually a part of it, is the charge of lack of poetic value. The reviewers again and again called *Don Juan* doggerel and insisted that it was tedious, poorly written, witless, spiritless, monotonous, digressive, heavy, dull, slovenly in versification, incoherent, pointless, unpoetical,

[45] Prothero, *op. cit.*, IV, 260. (To Thomas Moore. Venice, September 19, 1818.)

[46] *Ibid.*, VI, 155–56. (To John Murray. Genoa, December 25, 1822.)

trite, and even "destitute of the least glimmering of talent."

There is very little indeed in *Don Juan* that deserves the epithet "doggerel." It is doubtful if there was ever a poet, however great, who did not upon at least a few occasions lapse into something dangerously near doggerel. Certainly Byron is no more infallible than Milton or Wordsworth in this respect. But the designation of entire cantos of *Don Juan* as "mere doggerel" without exemplifying the accusation is unliterary criticism that scarcely merits serious attention. To be sure, Byron's too frequent carelessness and inattention to the details of versification are generally acknowledged. But that is not to say that the whole of Byron's serio-comic epic poem is "mere doggerel" and "destitute of the least glimmering of talent." Under Byron's skillful touch the eight-line stanza assumes a freedom and largeness and facility which it never before had exhibited in English. It sinks to an easy conversational tone, and, upon occasion, rises to the tone of high poetry. Byron demonstrates the exceeding flexibility and versatility of the stanza by making it the vehicle in turn of gaiety, sadness, comedy, seriousness, irony, facetiousness, sober meditation, and vigorous satire. He links stanza to stanza and obtains a continuity and a flowing effect that are remarkably adapted to narrative. In his hands *ottava rima* can become intimately colloquial and conversational or it can serve him as a facile medium for startling plunges from the serious to the ludicrous. It was such expert versification as this which the reviewers, motivated by the dominant critical prejudices of the day, branded as "slovenly" and anathematized as "doggerel."

There are passages in *Don Juan* that may with truth be spoken of as "tedious" and "too digressive," especially in the later cantos. But these are rare. The very nature of such writing is digression and discursion. The story, or plot, is a mere thread on which the beads of wit and satire are strung. Within the digressions are to be found most of Byron's acute observations, diverting innuendoes, witty sallies, and incisive thrusts of satire. It is the digressive and discursive nature of the serio-comic style which constitutes its peculiar charm and virtue.

There is no line in *Don Juan* that is "incoherent" and there are very few, if any, that are "pointless" or "meaningless." "Dullness," as Byron himself acknowledged, "is the only annihilator in such cases";[47] and he took care that dull moments should be rare in his poem. In the words of William Maginn, remonstrating with North for allowing *Don Juan* to be accused of dullness in *Blackwood's,* "Call things wicked, base, vile, obscene, blasphemous . . . . but never say that they are stupid when they are not. . . . . abuse Wickedness, but acknowledge Wit. . . . ."[48]

Let us next inquire if *Don Juan* is lacking in poetic value. What shall we say of the poetic truth which distinguishes *Don Juan* throughout? What shall we say of the many passages of true poetry written with ease and spirit? Of its melody? Of its harmonious interlinking of stanzas? Of its originality and variety of style? Of the intensity of Byron's absorption in the scene he is painting and of his identification of himself with his characters? Of his fire of imagination? Of his incomparable and tireless vigor? Of his passages of exquisite lyricism, of striking beauty, and of sublimity?

More specifically, attention should be called to Byron's penetrating analysis of the psychology of adolescent love (I, lxxxvi ff.); the exquisite stanzas enumerating the felicities of life (I, cxxii ff.); the riotous humor of the boudoir fiasco (I, cxxxvi ff.); the famous letter of Julia to

---

[47] Prothero, *op. cit.,* IV, 277–78. (To John Murray. Venice, January 25, 1819.)

[48] See above, p. 63.

Juan (I, cxcii ff.); the poetical commandments (I, cciv ff.);
the remarkable realism of the shipwreck episode (II,
xxiv ff.); the tender and idyllic beauty of the Haidée episode (II, cxxxix ff.); the ornate beauty of "Lambro's Return" (III, xxi ff.); the description of Haidée (III,
lxx ff.); the classic tone and spirit of the lyric, "The Isles
of Greece" (III, lxxxvi ff.); the devout reverence of the
"Ave Maria" stanzas (III, cii ff.); the moving description of Haidée's tragic death (IV, lvii ff.); the terse characterization of the members of the Italian opera-troupe
(IV, lxxx ff.); the episode of the slave market, with its
examples of the surpassing use of the octave for conversation (V, vi ff.); the luxurious description of the lovely
odalisques and of the sleeping beauties of the seraglio
(VI, xxix–lvi and lxiv–lxviii); the clever use in rhyme of
the names of the Russian generals (VII, xv–xvii); the
characterization of Marshal Suwarrow (VII, xlix ff.); the
vigorous and striking description of the "Siege of Ismail"
in Canto VIII; Juan's rescue of the little Turkish girl
(VIII, xci ff.); the resolute bravery of the Tartar Khan
and his five sons (VIII, civ ff.); the powerful satire of
war in Canto IX (i–xxi); the description of Catherine the
Great and her court (IX, xliii ff.); the description of the
appearance of England from the Channel and of the drive
from Canterbury to London (X, lxix ff.); the amusing
Shooter's Hill episode (XI, viii ff.); the famous *ubi sunt*
stanzas (XI, lxxvi ff.) and the equally famous "I have
seen" stanzas (XI, lxxxii ff.); the delectable whimsy inter-
mingled with incisive satire of Canto XII; the magnificent
poetry of the description of Norman Abbey (XIII, lv ff.);
and the sublime concluding stanza of Canto XV. In addi-
tion to all these specific passages of true poetry, there are
the manifold digressions, with their wealth of fancy,
whimsy, wit, innuendo, and subtle irony.

As for the validity or falsity of the charge of deliberate

intent to corrupt morals, one can decide only from the
internal evidence of *Don Juan*. Byron himself definitely
denied any evil intent[49] and insisted upon the satiric purpose of *Don Juan*.[50] And the internal evidence of the
poem itself establishes the sincerity of Byron's satiric purpose. A careful examination of the satiric elements of the
poem such as is provided below reveals their definitely
positive and constructive significance.

We come last to the accusation of revolutionary indoctrination in *Don Juan*. This is a valid stricture. *Don Juan*
is radical. Byron meant it to be. One of Byron's major
emphases in the latter cantos of the poem is revolutionary
indoctrination. Byron was one of the leading exponents
of the revolutionary philosophy of his epoch. Byron did
not hesitate to announce (VIII, cxxxv) his purpose unmis-
takably—

> For I will teach, if possible, the stones
> To rise against earth's tyrants . . . .

Of the eight major adverse criticisms of *Don Juan* made
by the contemporary reviewers, only this one—revolutionary indoctrination—is valid. And Byron would undoubtedly have regarded the accusation of radicalism as
complimentary rather than derogatory.

As for the alleged immoral tendency of *Don Juan*, it
has been grossly exaggerated by the contemporary reviewers. Although one must admit the modicum of truth in
the charge that *Don Juan* contains elements the tendency
of which is to exert a sensual influence upon susceptible
minds, this is not to acquiesce in the condemnation of *Don
Juan* as fundamentally immoral in tendency. Byron does
not stand guilty of equalizing virtues and vices, and he is
innocent of deliberate intent to corrupt morals. *Don Juan,*

[49] Prothero, *op. cit.*, IV, 279. (To John Murray. Venice, February 1, 1819.)

[50] *Ibid.*, VI, 155. (To John Murray. Genoa, December 25, 1822.)

as a satire of abuses in social institutions, is essentially moral in purpose and effect.

It is apparent that the contemporary reviewers failed to regard *Don Juan* in the spirit in which it was written. Flippancy of manner often disguises seriousness of purpose. The only test of Byron's real earnestness in *Don Juan* is the tendency of the work as a whole. This can be determined only by a close examination of the details in succession to discover their real trend. What does Byron praise and what does he blame? If after listing, as in the next section of this work, the various objects blamed and praised we can discern certain clear principles that seem to account for the selection of these particular objects, we shall have the real criterion of purpose, divested of the superficial, clever persiflage which may disguise it to the casual eye.

The underlying causes of the failure of the reviewers to regard *Don Juan* in its true light are apparent. The most obvious characteristic of periodical reviewing during the second and third decades of the nineteenth century was the pronounced political and moral bias of the critics. This bias was motivated by two almost hysterical fears: religious fear and bigotry, and the fear of political revolution. The periodical press was extremely concerned about religious and political defection. These fears affected not only the general tone and policy of the periodicals but their theory and practice of literary criticism as well. As Professor Newman Ivey White has well said, "A glance through the literary journals of this troubled period will reveal at once how greatly the special fears of the times warped criticism in the direction of considering literature largely from an unliterary point of view."[51]

When we remember that Lord Byron was not only a

[51] Newman Ivey White, *The Unextinguished Hearth; Shelley and His Contemporary Critics* (Duke University Press, 1938), p. 10.

liberal in politics but a radical, and that he was suspected, however mistakenly, of atheism, it is not hard to understand why the contemporary periodical criticism of his *Don Juan* was preponderantly adverse. Byron's critics were not blind to his genius; they were afraid of it.

III
BYRON'S REACTION TO THE REVIEWS

Byron's reaction to the contemporary periodical criticism of *Don Juan* is clearly revealed in his allusions to the reviews in his letters and journals and in the subsequent cantos of the poem itself.

That Byron expected criticism of *Don Juan* is obvious. In the first canto of the poem (stanzas ccvii and ccix), composed in September 1818, he wrote:

> If any person should presume to assert
>   This story is not moral, first, I pray,
> That they will not cry out before they're hurt,
>   Then that they'll read it o'er again, and say,
> (But, doubtless, nobody will be so pert),
>   That this is not a moral tale, though gay;
> Besides, in Canto Twelfth, I mean to show
> The very place where wicked people go.
>
> .   .   .   .
>
> The public approbation I expect,
>   And beg they'll take my word about the moral,
> Which I with their amusement will connect
>   (So children cutting teeth receive a coral);

He also feigns (I, ccix) to have bribed a British review and adds (ccxi):

> I think that with this holy new alliance
>   I may ensure the public, and defy
> All other magazines of art or science,
>   Daily, or monthly, or three monthly; I

> Have not essay'd to multiply their clients,
>   Because they tell me 'twere in vain to try,
> And that the Edinburgh Review and Quarterly
>   Treat a dissenting author very martyrly.

And again, at the end of the canto (stanza ccxxi), and with his tongue still in his cheek, addressing the "gentle reader" Byron promises to write no more of the poem if "this short sample" is not understood:

> We meet again, if we should understand
>   Each other; and if not, I shall not try
> Your patience further than by this short sample—
>   'Twere well if others follow'd my example.

These expressions indicate that Byron was at least not certain of a favorable reception for *Don Juan*. Toward the end of the poem (XV, lx) he says he has foreseen that the work would meet with disapproval.

> I say, in my slight way I may proceed
>   To play upon the surface of humanity.
> I write the world, nor care if the world read,
>   At least for this I cannot spare its vanity.
> My Muse hath bred, and still perhaps may breed
>   More foes by this same scroll: when I began it, I
> Thought that it might turn out so—*now* I *know* it,
>   But still I am, or was, a pretty poet.

But Byron could hardly have foreseen the severity of the censure which *Don Juan* encountered. On January 25, 1819, when he was completing a second canto (not having waited, as he had promised, to ascertain whether or not the "gentle reader" understood Canto I), he wrote Murray[52] defending his poem against the charges of indecency and rakishness alleged by his "cursed puritanical committee" and protesting that,

[52] Prothero, *op. cit.*, IV, 277–78. (To John Murray. Venice, January 25, 1819.)

If the poem has poetry, it would stand; if not, fall . . . .
Dullness is the only annihilator in such cases. As to the Cant of
the day, I despise it, as I have ever done all its finical fashions,
which become you as paint became the Antient Britons. If you
admit this prudery, you must omit half Ariosto, Shakespeare,
Beaumont, Fletcher, Massinger, Ford, all the Charles Second
writers; in short, *something* of most who have written before
Pope and are worth reading, and much of Pope himself . . . .

And again on February 1 Byron wrote to Murray[53] re-
iterating his denial of the immorality of *Don Juan* and
maintaining it to be "the most moral of poems":

If they had told me the poetry was bad, I would have acqui-
esced; but they say the contrary and then talk to me about morality
—the first time I ever heard the word from anybody who was
not a rascal that used it for a purpose. I maintain that it is the
most moral of poems; but if people won't discover the moral,
that is their fault, not mine.

I quote these letters to Murray in order to emphasize
the fact that Byron not only expected criticism but foresaw
the nature of the criticism. There is, however, no indica-
tion that he anticipated the virulence of it. Murray's alarm
about the hue and cry which the publication of the poem
would raise elicited from Byron this astute response:

Methinks I see you with a long face about *Don Juan*, anticipating the outcry and the scalping reviews that will ensue; *all that*
is my affair: do you think I do not forsee [*sic*] all this as well as
you?[54]

It is evident that Byron realized that considerable opposition would greet the first cantos of *Don Juan* but this did
not deter him from publishing it. On the contrary, he
appeared to anticipate the forthcoming conflict with relish.
The first two cantos of *Don Juan* appeared on July 15,

[53] *Ibid.*, IV, 279. (To John Murray. Venice, February 1, 1819.)
[54] *Ibid.*, IV, 294–95. (To John Murray. Venice, May 6, 1819.)

1819. Two weeks later, but before he had heard of the reception of the poem, Byron wrote Murray: "You will see me defend myself gaily—that is if I happen to be in Spirits . . . . You may perhaps see some good tossing and goring . . . . Come what may, I never will flatter the millions' canting in any shape . . . ."[55]

Soon the storm of English fury reached Byron's ears in Italy. *Don Juan* was called obscene, impious, and studiously lewd, and Byron was accused of deliberate intent to corrupt morals and undermine the bulwarks of society. But Byron's courage did not falter and, keeping up a bold front, he wrote to Murray, "Keep the anonymous. . . . . It helps what fun there may be; but if the matter grows serious about *Juan* . . . . *own that I am the author*. I will never shrink."[56]

And although Byron, undaunted, busied himself with the composition of a third canto, he was by no means insensible to the hostility of the reviewers. Shortly after being virulently attacked in *Blackwood's*, in August 1819, for his "satire on the character and manners of his wife,"[57] Byron wrote less confidently to his publisher, "I have finished the third Canto of *D. J.*, but the things I have read and heard discourage all further publication—at least for the present."[58] Furthermore, he had got the impression from Murray that the cantos had not sold well because of the alleged indecency of the poem. Considerably irritated by this news he again defended his poem against the charge of indecency in a letter to Hoppner.

---

[55] Prothero, *op. cit.*, IV, 326–27. (To John Murray. Ravenna, August 1, 1819.)

[56] *Ibid.*, IV, 348. (To John Murray. Bologna, August 24, 1819.)

[57] "*Don Juan.* Cantos I–II," in *Blackwood's Edinburgh Magazine*, V (August 1819), 512–18.

[58] Prothero, *op. cit.*, IV, 384. (To John Murray. Venice, October 10, 1819.)

I understand the outcry was beyond everything—pretty Cant for people who read *Tom Jones,* and *Roderick Random,* and the *Bath Guide,* and Ariosto, and Dryden, and Pope, to say nothing of *Little's Poems.* Of course I refer to the *morality* of those works, and not to any pretension of mine to compete with them in anything but decency.[59]

Let us now turn again to *Don Juan* and examine the allusions to periodical criticism in the third and fourth cantos, which Byron completed in February 1820.

Byron reports (IV, xcvii) hearing that people take exception to the first two cantos of his poem "having too much truth":

> Here I might enter on a chaste description,
>   Having withstood temptation in my youth,
> But hear that several people take exception
>   At the first two books having too much truth;
> Therefore I'll make Don Juan leave the ship soon,
>   Because the publisher declares, in sooth,
> Through needles' eyes it easier for the camel is
> To pass, than those two cantos into families.

He continues (xcviii):

> 'Tis all the same to me; I'm fond of yielding,
>   And therefore leave them to the purer page
> Of Smollett, Prior, Ariosto, Fielding,
>   Who say strange things for so correct an age;
> I once had great alacrity in wielding
>   My pen, and liked poetic war to wage,
> And recollect the time when all this cant
> Would have provoked remarks which now it shan't.

But beneath this banter is real earnestness. His *Don Juan,* Byron felt, was no more deserving of censure on the score of morals than the productions of the other authors he mentions. Neither was his mood as suited to the waging

---

[59] *Ibid.,* IV, 366–67. (To Richard B. Hoppner. Venice, October 28, 1819.)

of "poetic war" as it had been in the hot-headed days of *English Bards and Scotch Reviewers*. Although anger and the desire for retaliation were not unfamiliar to Byron at this stage of the *Don Juan* controversy, they were secondary to his dominant mood of contempt for what he characterized as the "cant" and "hypocrisy" of the reviews. And this contempt was coupled with a firm confidence that in *Don Juan* he had written to the top of his ability, and that it would stand or fall on its own merits.[60]

He may have had *Blackwood's* attack of August 1819 in mind as he wrote stanza cvii of Canto IV, protesting against the censure visited upon poets for revealing "as in a glass" their inmost passions "in such colours that they seem to live":

> If in the course of such a life as was
>   At once adventurous and contemplative,
> Men who partake all passions as they pass,
>   Acquire the deep and bitter power to give
> Their images again as in a glass,
>   And in such colours that they seem to live;
> You may do right forbidding them to show 'em,
> But spoil (I think) a very pretty poem.

The third, fourth, and fifth cantos of *Don Juan* were published together on August 8, 1821. Among the abuse these cantos elicited was a charge of plagiarism. Concerning this charge Byron wrote to Murray on August 23, 1821: "Almost all *Don Juan* is *real* life, either my own, or from people I knew. . . . . *I* laugh at such charges, convinced that no writer ever borrowed less, or made his materials more his own."[61] And with regard to specific

[60] Prothero, *op. cit.*, V, 351–52. (To John Murray. Ravenna, August 31, 1821.)

[61] *Ibid.*, V, 346–47. (To John Murray. Ravenna, August 23, 1821.)

charges about his indebtedness for the shipwreck scene Byron said in the same letter:

I think that I told both you and Mr. Hobhouse, years ago, that [there] was not a single circumstance of it not taken from *fact;* not, indeed, from any *single* shipwreck, but all from *actual* facts of different wrecks . . . . by the way, much of the description of the *furniture,* in Canto 3rd, is taken from *Tully's Tripoli* (pray *note this*), and the rest from my own observation.[62]

On September 4, 1821, in a letter to John Murray, Byron confessed that the outcry against *Don Juan* was irritating him and he requested that no periodicals whatsoever be sent him:

. . . . If they [the articles in the reviews] regard myself, they tend to increase *Egotism;* if favourable, I do not deny that the praise *elates,* and if unfavourable, that the abuse *irritates*— . . . . Therefore let me hear none of your provocations. . . . . I merely request to be left in ignorance. . . . . You will say, "to what tends all this?" I will answer *That;*—to keep my mind *free and unbiased* by all paltry and personal irritabilities of praise or censure;—to let my genius take its natural direction. . . . .[63]

This wise decision of Byron's—"to let my genius take its natural direction"—is indicative of Byron's increasing assurance that in *Don Juan* he had found his true vein. It is a reiteration of the conviction he had expressed in a letter to Murray a few weeks earlier when acknowledging the receipt of a parcel of the newly published cantos: "I have read over the poem carefully, and I tell you *it is poetry* . . . . time will show that I am not in this instance mistaken."[64] Byron's critical acuteness with regard to *Don*

[62] The italics are Byron's. Richard Tully, Consul at Tripoli 1783–93, wrote a *Narrative of a Ten Years' Residence at the Court of Tripoli,* published in 1816. See *Don Juan,* Canto III, stanzas lxvii–lxix.

[63] Prothero, *op. cit.,* V, 373–75. (To John Murray. Ravenna, September 24, 1821.)

[64] *Ibid.,* V, 351–52. (To John Murray. Ravenna, August 31, 1821.)

Juan[65] and his determination not to allow his genius to be deflected from its "natural direction," either by calumny or by excessive praise, is clearly evidenced in a letter to Douglas Kinnaird, written February 25, 1822, in which he said:

My object is not *immediate* popularity in my present productions, which are written on a different system from the rage of the day. But, *mark what I say;* that the time will come when these will be preferred to any I have before written:—it is not from the cry or hubbub of a month that these things are to be decided upon.[66]

As Nicolson has pointed out, Byron, toward the end of his brief career, came to pride himself on possessing no illusions about his poetry. He came to despise his own earlier, romantic manner and to regard *Don Juan* alone as possessing some claim to immortality. Nicolson quotes Byron as having once said to Shelley:

As long as I wrote the exaggerated nonsense which has corrupted the public taste, they applauded me to the very echo; and now that I have composed within these three or four years some things which I "should not willingly let die," the whole herd snort and grumble, and return to wallow in their mire.[67]

Byron's next allusion in *Don Juan* to contemporary criticism of the poem is in a figure of speech (X, iv) likening *Don Juan* to a boat which has sailed, undaunted by the fury of the waves, through waters where many ships have foundered.

[65] Ethel C. Mayne points out that Byron's sound self-criticism with regard to *Don Juan* is in strong contrast to his "extraordinary blindness to his true characteristics" in every other self-criticism. See Mayne, *op. cit.*, p. 356.

[66] Prothero, *op. cit.*, VI, 25. (To the Hon. Douglas Kinnaird. Pisa, February 25, 1822.)

[67] Harold Nicolson, *Byron, the Last Journey* (London, 1924), p. 43.

In the wind's eye I have sail'd, and sail; but for
    The stars, I own my telescope is dim;
But at the least I have shunn'd the common shore,
    And leaving land far out of sight, would skim
The ocean of eternity: the roar
    Of breakers has not daunted my slight, trim,
But *still* sea-worthy skiff; and she may float
Where ships have founder'd, as doth many a boat.

Again, in the same canto (X, xvi), Byron forgives
Francis Jeffrey for his censure of *Don Juan* in the *Edinburgh* and owns that "on the whole" Jeffrey has acted
most nobly:

And all our little feuds, at least all *mine*,
    Dear Jeffrey, once my most redoubted foe
(As far as rhyme and criticism combine
    To make such puppets of us things below),
Are over: Here's a health to "Auld Lang Syne!"
    I do not know you, and may never know
Your face—but you have acted on the whole
Most nobly, and I own it from my soul.

In Canto XI (lxii–lxiii) Byron expresses his scorn of
reviewers:

This is the literary *lower* empire,
    Where the praetorian bands take up the matter;—
A "dreadful trade," like his who "gathers samphire,"
    The insolent soldiery to soothe and flatter,
With the same feelings as you'd coax a vampire.
    Now, were I once at home, and in good satire,
I'd try conclusions with those Janizaries,
And show them *what* an intellectual war is.

I think I know a trick or two, would turn
    Their flanks;—but it is hardly worth my while
With such small gear to give myself concern:
    Indeed I've not the necessary bile;

> My natural temper's really aught but stern,
>   And even my Muse's worst reproof's a smile;
> And then she drops a brief and modern curtsy,
>   And glides away, assured she never hurts ye.

Byron takes another thrust at critics who allege that he equalizes virtues and vices in his *Don Juan*. Canto XIII opens with these words:

> I now mean to be serious;—it is time,
>   Since laughter now-a-days is deem'd too serious;
> A jest at Vice by Virtue's call'd a crime,
>   And critically held as deleterious:

The last reference in *Don Juan* to the "critics" occurs in Canto XV. Here (xxii) Byron summarizes his contemptuous attitude toward his critics by saying:

> I meant to make this poem very short,
>   But now I can't tell where it may not run.
> No doubt, if I had wish'd to pay my court
>   To critics, or to hail the *setting* sun
> Of tyranny of all kinds, my concision
> Were more;—but I was born for opposition.

One of Byron's latest allusions to English periodical criticism of his *Don Juan* was in a conversation with Lady Blessington at Genoa in the spring of 1823, shortly before he embarked upon the Greek adventure. He does not refer specifically to the acrimonious reviews of *Don Juan* in this conversation, but it is more than likely that he had them in mind. He said:

> I have often thought of writing a book to be filled with all the charges brought against me in England; it would make an interesting folio, with my notes, and might serve posterity as a proof of the charity, good-nature, and candour of Christian England in the nineteenth century.[68]

---

[68] Blessington, *op. cit.*, pp. 275–76.

I conclude this discussion with a summary of the effect of the contemporary periodical criticism upon *Don Juan*. Before the publication of the poem, Byron foresaw that it would be censured on the score of morals. But from the jesting nature of his remarks at this time, I infer that he did not foresee either the extent or the degree of severity of the criticism that was to follow. However, he was expecting, even anticipating, opposition. As he said, he was "born for opposition," and he seemed to relish the prospect of it in this instance.

When the storm of hostility broke he was apparently surprised at its virulency. But he did not falter. The major accusation was "immorality," and his resolute response was "Cant!" He maintained that his poem was no more liable to this charge than the works of many accepted and "classic" authors. Again and again he defended *Don Juan* against this charge—even asserting that it was "the most moral of poems" and that if people would not discover the moral it was their fault and not his.

Although at times harassed by the severity of the hostile criticism of *Don Juan*, Byron's dominant reaction was contempt for the "hypocrisy" of his critics and determination to ignore both their censure and their praise. This determination was the result of a profound conviction that in *Don Juan* his genius was taking its "natural direction" and finding its highest and most complete expression.

The one exception to Byron's consistent attitude of contempt for and deliberate indifference to contemporary criticism is his admission that Francis Jeffrey had, "on the whole," acted "most nobly" in his treatment of *Don Juan* in *The Edinburgh Review* for February 1822. But it is to be remembered that the severity of Jeffrey's strictures on *Don Juan* is palliated by his generous praise of the poetic merits of the poem. Jeffrey's review was one of the most tolerant and just of all the contemporary reviews of *Don*

Juan, and Byron was not blind to this. Furthermore, Jeffrey had defended Byron against the most damning of all the charges preferred against him—that of deliberate intent to corrupt morals. Jeffrey had maintained that Lord Byron was not a resolvedly wicked man.

In short, of the several major charges brought against Byron and his *Don Juan* by the periodical reviewers, Byron's reaction focuses on two: immorality, and lack of poetic value. He consistently denies the immoral tendency of *Don Juan* and insists upon its poetic worth.

It would seem, then, that *Don Juan* was not affected in any essential way or to any noteworthy degree by the periodical criticism which it elicited. This criticism, as we have seen, was motivated primarily by the dominant political and religious prejudices of the day, rather than by the principles of true literary criticism. Byron fully realized this and branded the censure as "Cant!" True to the intuition that in social satire he was pursuing his highest bent, he would not allow the censure to deter him from his purpose in *Don Juan.* The noteworthy increase in seriousness of the later cantos of *Don Juan* was due not to the contemporary criticism of the poem but to the maturation of Byron's essentially satiric genius.

Chapter Three

THE SIGNIFICANCE OF
DON JUAN

I

LORD BYRON AS A SATIRIST

𝕿HERE has been no adequate treatment of the significance of *Don Juan* as a satire. Among the best brief discussions of the general satiric character of the poem are those of John Morley, George Brandes, Paul Elmer More, and Claude M. Fuess. But these discussions do not provide a detailed and analytical examination of the objects of Byron's satire, nor do they furnish a critical evaluation of the poem.

Fuess, in his study of Byron as a satirist in verse, praises Byron's extraordinary satiric power but maintains that Byron's "broader philosophic satire . . . . is essentially shallow and cynical."[1] Byron, he asserts, "took no positive attitude towards any of the great problems of existence."[2] Now this assertion seems unsupported by the facts, which are as follows:

Byron's poetical career falls into three rather clearly defined periods: the early period, from about 1809, when his *English Bards and Scotch Reviewers* appeared, to 1812, the year in which the first two cantos of *Childe Harold*

---

[1] Claude M. Fuess, *Lord Byron as a Satirist in Verse* (New York, 1912), p. 215. Quoted by permission of Columbia University Press.
[2] *Ibid.*, p. 179.

were published; the middle period, from 1812 to his final departure from England in 1816; and the final period, from 1816 to the year of his death, 1824.

Byron early manifested his bent for satire. His most notable production during this first period was his vigorously satirical *English Bards and Scotch Reviewers*, conveying his strong and angry reaction to the severe censure of his own earlier schoolboy verse, "Hours of Idleness" (1807). As Calvert has pointed out, Byron modeled this 1809 satire largely upon the "Baviad" and the "Maeviad" of William Gifford, the last strong satirist of the eighteenth century.[3] As such, Byron's first important satire is a continuation of the neoclassic satiric tradition of Pope and Dryden. The reasons for Byron's sympathy with the classic tradition are clearly set forth by Calvert in his chapter on Byron as "The Man of Sense."[4] Among the reasons which he suggests, one of the most convincing is that the Augustan tradition appealed to Byron because it reflected "the self-assurance and conscious self-mastery of a ruling class used to the sense of control, and offered to the artist an intelligent, critical audience, sympathetic to qualities like its own."[5]

English Bards and Scotch Reviewers, Byron's major achievement in the neoclassic manner, occupies an important place in the history of English satire, being the last notable English satire in the heroic-couplet measure.[6] Quite in keeping with the neoclassic tradition, this satire is personal and violent.

However, as Byron's satiric genius matured, he developed more and more the mocking and ironic manner of the

[3] William J. Calvert, *Byron: Romantic Paradox* (University of North Carolina Press, Chapel Hill, 1935), p. 38.

[4] *Ibid.*, pp. 38–73.   [5] *Ibid.*, p. 52.

[6] Hugh Walker, *English Satire and Satirists* (New York, 1925), p. 263.

Italian burlesque poets. The major poem of his final period was his seriocomic satire, *Don Juan.*

The point I wish to make here is that the major poetical production of Byron's early period, as well as of his final period, is satire. As I have already noted, his poetical career may be said to begin and end with satire. His remarks on this subject to the Countess of Blessington throw light on the springs of his satiric inclination:

> When anyone attacks me, on the spur of the moment I sit down and write all the *mechanceté* that comes into my head; and as some of these sallies have merit, they amuse me, and are too good to be torn or burned, and so are kept, and see the light long after the feeling that dictated them has subsided. All my malice evaporates in the effusions of my pen.[7]

Don Juan, unique and extraordinary as it undeniably is, is not to be regarded as unrelated to Byron's earlier satires. Like all of Byron's satire, whether neoclassic or seriocomic, *Don Juan* is the inevitable fruitage of Byron's essential satiric genius. When, as a youth, he was wounded by the severity of the critics, he responded with *English Bards and Scotch Reviewers.* Now, as an exile from England, wounded not by individuals but by society, his response was not personal vituperation but social satire.

As we have seen, Byron very definitely avowed his purpose in *Don Juan* to be "a *Satire* on *abuses* of the present states of Society, and not an eulogy of vice . . . ."[8] Similarly, Byron responded to Kennedy's question concerning his purpose in *Don Juan,* saying that it was

> . . . . to remove the cloke, which the manners and maxims of society throw over their secret sins, and shew them to the world

---

[7] Blessington, *op. cit.,* p. 268.
[8] Prothero, *op. cit.,* VI, 155–56. (To John Murray. Genoa, December 25, 1822.)

as they really are. You have not been so much in high and noble life as I have been; but if you had fully entered into it, and seen what was going on, you would have felt convinced that it was time to unmask the specious hypocrisy, and shew it in its native colors.[9]

Since, then, Byron distinctly asserted his satiric purpose in *Don Juan*, let us study the poem itself to see if Byron's statement of purpose is supported by his performance. The purpose of the study is twofold: first, to distinguish the objects of Byron's satire in *Don Juan*; and, second, to evaluate the positive significance of Byron's satire.

Byron satirizes individuals, England and things English, and social institutions and modern society in general. In presenting them I shall begin with the satire of individuals, as the least significant of the group, and reserve last place for the most important, the satire of institutions and of modern society. This is the progressive order of their relative importance, judging from the attention and emphasis which Byron gives them.

II

SATIRE OF INDIVIDUALS

There are eight individuals to whom satiric reference is frequently made in *Don Juan*. In the diminishing order of the respective attention which they receive from Byron, they are:

Robert Southey	The Duke of Wellington
Catherine of Russia	(Wellesley)
Castlereagh (Lord Lon-	Lady Byron
donderry)	King George IV
William Wordsworth	Samuel Taylor Coleridge

[9] James Kennedy, *Conversations on Religion with Lord Byron and Others* (London, 1830), p. 163.

The following individuals likewise are satirized but less frequently than those of the first group:

Lord Brougham   Marshal Suwarrow
Lady Caroline Lamb   Napoleon
Joanna Southcote   Rev. T. R. Malthus
          Sir Samuel Romilly

And there is a third group of individuals at each of whom Byron takes at least one satiric fling:

William Sotheby   Barry Cornwall
Queen Caroline   Beau Brummell
John Murray   Samuel Whitbread
Prince Potemkin   Frances Wedderburn
General Markow   Webster
William Pitt   William Mitford
Queen Elizabeth   Lord Eldon
Reverend G. Croly   Izaak Walton
Henry Hart Milman   Sidney Smith
John Keats   Sir William Curtis[10]

To the last list may be added the names of five people on whom speculation fixes as the real individuals disguised behind the false names of the house guests at Norman Abbey (Canto XIII). According to E. H. Coleridge, they are: James Mackintosh, Sir George Prevost, John Philpot Curran, Thomas Lord Erskine, and Richard Sharp.[11]

Byron detested Southey for several reasons. Southey was Poet-Laureate of England, and that in itself to Byron spelled servility and insincerity. Then, too, Southey was a Tory. And the combination of Poet-Laureate and Tory was to Byron most odious. Furthermore, Southey was identified in Byron's mind with the "Lakers," Wordsworth

[10] This list is illustrative rather than exhaustive. Ambiguous and obscure allusions are omitted.

[11] Coleridge, *op. cit.*, VI, 507–11.

and Coleridge, who mumbled metaphysical vagaries beside their rural ponds. Southey attacked Byron and "The Satanic School" in the preface to his "Vision of Judgment" (1821). And, lastly, Byron was under the impression that Southey had spread the rumor in England that he and Shelley had been in a "league of Incest" in Switzerland with Mary Godwin and Claire Clairmont.[12]

To Southey Byron addressed his fierce and violent "Dedication" of *Don Juan*. Stanzas xvi–xvii read:

. . . .

> Europe has slaves, allies, kings, armies still,
> And Southey lives to sing them very ill.
>
> Meantime, Sir Laureate, I proceed to dedicate,
>   In honest simple verse, this song to you.
> And, if in flattering strains I do not predicate,
>   'Tis that I still retain my "buff and blue";
> My politics as yet are all to educate:
>   Apostasy's so fashionable, too,
> To keep *one* creed's a task grown quite Herculean:
> Is it not so, my Tory, Ultra-Julian?

Byron's first allusion to Southey in the body of the poem is in the "poetical commandments" in Canto I (ccv):

> Thou shalt believe in Milton, Dryden, Pope;
>   Thou shalt not set up Wordsworth, Coleridge, Southey;
> Because the first is crazed beyond all hope,
>   The second drunk, the third so quaint and mouthy:

A little farther on (ccxxii) he quotes Southey in derision and exclaims:

> The first four rhymes are Southey's, every line:
> For God's sake, reader! take them not for mine!

[12] Prothero, *op. cit.*, IV, 271 ff. (To John Murray. Venice, November 24, 1818.)

In Canto III there are three vigorous stanzas (lxxix–lxxxi) satirizing Southey as a sycophant, opportunist, and turncoat. Byron, pretending to describe an "Eastern anti-jacobin," draws a portrait of Southey which is very much like the Southey of Byron's "Vision of Judgment" (xcvii–xcix):

> He praised the present, and abused the past,
>   Reversing the good custom of old days,
> An Eastern anti-jacobin at last
>   He turn'd, preferring pudding to *no* praise—
> For some few years his lot had been o'ercast
>   By his seeming independent in his lays,
> But now he sung the Sultan and the Pacha
> With truth like Southey, and with verse like Crashaw.
>
> He was a man who had seen many changes,
>   And always changed as true as any needle;
> His polar star being one which rather ranges,
>   And not the fix'd—he knew the way to wheedle:
> So vile he 'scaped the doom which oft avenges;
>   And being fluent (save indeed when fee'd ill),
> He lied with such a fervour of intention—
> There was no doubt he earn'd his laureate pension.

Byron ridicules Southey's didacticism in Canto III (stanza xciii), and in the ensuing stanza (xciv) labels him "convict" and "renegado." "Such names," says Byron, referring to Wordsworth, Coleridge, and Southey,

>   at present cut a convict figure,
>   The very Botany Bay in moral geography;
> Their loyal treason, renegado rigour,
>   Are good manure for their more bare biography . . . .

And, again, Byron gibes at Southey's wordiness, suggesting (III, xcvii) that an "epic" may be expected from Southey every spring:

> I know that what our neighbors call *"longueurs,"*
>   (We've not so good a *word*, but have the *thing*,
> In that complete perfection which insures
>   An epic from Bob Southey every Spring—)
> Form not the true temptation which allures
>   The reader; but 'twould not be hard to bring
> Some fine examples of the *epopée*,
>   To prove its grand ingredient is *ennui*.

Byron's contempt for Southey prompts these harsh words in Canto X (xiii):

> This were the worst desertion:—renegadoes,
>   Even shuffling Southey, that incarnate lie,
> Would scarcely join again the "reformadoes,"
>   Whom he forsook to fill the laureate's sty:
> And honest men from Iceland to Barbadoes,
>   Whether in Caledon or Italy,
> Should not veer round with every breath, nor seize
> To pain, the moment when you cease to please.

Byron plays another variation of the theme of Southey's servility when he remarks (X, xxxvii) that monarchs shrink from rhymes, "save such as Southey can afford to give." In a clever stanza in which (XI, lvi) he compares his own fancied poetical decline to the decline of Napoleon, Byron suggests that he may eventually go to "some lonely isle" with "turncoat Southey" for his "turnkey Lowe." His last fling at Southey in *Don Juan* occurs in Canto XIV (lviii); in casting about for a similitude for his hatred of "a motive," Byron here lists, among others, "a laureate's ode."[13]

The next individual against whom Byron directs the full force of his satiric power is Catherine of Russia, the

---

[13] While *Don Juan* was appearing, Byron replied to Southey's preface to his "Vision of Judgment" with a powerful satiric attack on Southey in "The Vision of Judgment" (1821) beside which Southey's preface appears insignificant.

"queen of queans" (VI, xcvi) and "greatest of all sovereigns and w——s" (VI, xcii). Byron first (VII, lxiv) inveighs against the military ruthlessness of "the Christian Empress Catherine"; then (IX, xxix) he makes the charge more telling:

> Don Juan, who had shone in the late slaughter,
>   Was left upon his way with the despatch,
> Where blood was talked of as we would of water;
>   And carcasses that lay as thick as thatch
> O'er silenced cities, merely served to flatter
>   Fair Catherine's pastime—who look'd on the match
> Between these nations as a main of cocks,
> Wherein she liked her own to stand like rocks.

Catherine's bloodthirsty ambition is vigorously satirized in the stanzas describing her reactions as she reads (IX, lix–lx) the despatch in which Suwarrow reports the capture of Ismail:

> Great joy was here, or rather joys: the first
>   Was a ta'en city, thirty thousand slain.
> Glory and triumph o'er her aspect burst,
>   As an East Indian sunrise on the main.
> These quench'd a moment her ambition's thirst—
>   So Arab deserts drink in summer's rain:
> In vain!—As fall the dews on quenchless sands,
> Blood only serves to wash Ambition's hands!
>
> Her next amusement was more fanciful;
>   She smiled at mad Suwarrow's rhymes, who threw
> Into a Russian couplet rather dull
>   The whole gazette of thousands whom he slew.
> Her third was feminine enough to annul
>   The shudder which runs naturally through
> Our veins, when things call'd sovereigns think it best
> To kill, and generals turn it into jest.

The despatch itself (VIII, cxxxiii), which Suwarrow wrote with bloody hands while the roar of cannons was "scarce allay'd," links Catherine's name with God!

> Suwarrow now was conqueror—a match
>   For Timour or for Zinghis in his trade.
> While mosques and streets, beneath his eyes, like thatch
>   Blazed, and the cannon's roar was scarce allay'd,
> With bloody hands he wrote his first despatch;
>   And here exactly follows what he said:—
> "Glory to *God* and to the Empress!" (*Powers
> Eternal! such names mingled!*) "Ismail's ours."

Catherine's despotism Byron denounces in Canto IX (xxiii):

> For me, I deem an absolute autocrat
> *Not* a barbarian, but much worse than that.

Byron next (IX, lxii–lxiii) satirizes Catherine's lasciviousness—her amours are as ruthless and exacting as her military operations:

> She could repay each amatory look you lent
>   With interest, and in turn was wont with rigour
> To exact of Cupid's bills the full amount
>   At sight, nor would permit you to discount.
>
> With her the latter, though at times convenient,
>   Was not so necessary; for they tell
> That she was handsome, and though fierce *look'd* lenient,
>   And always used her favourites too well.
> If once beyond her boudoir's precincts in ye went,
>   Your "fortune" was in a fair way "to swell
> A man" (as Giles says); for though she would widow all
> Nations, she liked man as an individual.

Catherine's insatiable amorousness that requires one paramour after another is slurred in these stanzas (IX, xlvii–xlviii):

Besides, the empress sometimes liked a boy,
And had just buried the fair-faced Lanskoi.

No wonder then that Yermoloff, or Momonoff,
    Or Scherbatoff, or any other *off*
Or *on*, might dread her majesty had not room enough
    Within her bosom (which was not too tough)
For a new flame; a thought to cast of gloom enough
    Along the aspect, whether smooth or rough,
Of him who, in the language of his station,
Then held that "high official situation."

Byron does not hesitate to expose Catherine's colossal
concupiscence (IX, liv–lvii):

And Catherine, who loved all things (save her lord,
    Who was gone to his place), and pass'd for much,
Admiring those (by dainty dames abhorr'd)
    Gigantic gentlemen, yet had a touch
Of sentiment; and he she most adored
    Was the lamented Lanskoi, who was such
A lover as had cost her many a tear,
And yet but made a middling grenadier.

Oh thou "teterrima causa" of all "belli"—
    Thou gate of life and death—thou nondescript!
Whence is our exit and our entrance, well I
    May pause in pondering how all souls are dipt
In thy perennial fountain: how man *fell* I
    Know not, since knowledge saw her branches stript
Of her first fruit; but how he falls and rises,
Since, thou hast settled beyond all surmises.

Some call thee "the worst cause of war," but I
    Maintain thou art the *best:* for after all
From thee we come, to thee we go, and why
    To get at thee not batter down a wall,

Or waste a world? since no one can deny
    Thou dost replenish worlds both great and small:
With, or without thee, all things at a stand
Are, or would be, thou sea of life's dry land?

Catherine, who was the grand epitome
    Of that great cause of war, or peace, or what
You please (it causes all things which be,
    So you may take your choice of this or that)—
Catherine, I say, was very glad to see
    The handsome herald, on whose plumage sat
Victory; and, pausing as she saw him kneel
With his despatch, forgot to break the seal.

This whole episode of the Russian court (Canto IX) paints vividly and unsparingly Catherine's moral debasement. And the Empress, smitten with "love or lust" for Juan, makes him (X, lxxvii) her paramour:

Well, we won't analyse—our story must
    Tell for itself: the sovereign was smitten,
Juan much flatter'd by her love, or lust;—
    I cannot stop to alter words once written,
And the two are so mix'd with human dust,
    That he who *names one*, both perchance may hit on:
But in such matters Russia's mighty empress
Behaved no better than a common sempstress.

In Canto X, stanza xxix, Byron refers to Catherine as "an old woman," and thus emphasizes the incongruity of her conduct and age. Elsewhere (IX, lxxx) he says she had "a cursed taste for war" and was not "the best wife, unless we call such Clytemnestra." And in an earlier canto (VIII, lxviii), with the same thing in mind, he ridicules "Catherine's boudoir at three-score."

As the Russian court episode continues (X, xliv), the demands of "Russia's royal harlot" exhaust Juan; he sickens, and the doctors prescribe travel. Catherine, whose "climacteric teased her like her teens," was so distressed by Juan's departure that "she could not find at first a fit successor" (X, xlvii). But, fortunately, before twenty-four hours had elapsed, a candidate was chosen and Catherine was enabled to "taste next night a quiet slumber" (X, xlviii).

Byron indulges in one more slurring sarcasm about Catherine. A "monstrous diamond" worn by Juan, now an envoy from Russia to England, draws much observation from the English. It was a jewel, Byron tells us, which Catherine, in "love or brandy's fervent fermentation," had bestowed upon Juan, and "to say truth, it had been fairly earn'd" (XI, xxxix).[14]

Byron then attacks Viscount Castlereagh, the Marquess of Londonderry. Byron regarded Castlereagh as the worst of ministers and as a sentimental oligarch. He maintained that, as a minister, Londonderry was the "most despotic in intention, and the weakest in intellect, that ever tyrannised over a country."[15]

Castlereagh is viciously lampooned by Byron in the "Dedication" to *Don Juan*, stanzas xi to xvi. The first of Byron's two abusive epithets for Castlereagh appears here —"The intellectual eunuch Castlereagh" (xi)—the other well-known one is "Carotid-artery-cutting-Castlereagh" (X, lix). Byron calls him ("Dedication," xii) a

> cold-blooded, smooth-faced, placid miscreant!
> Dabbling its sleek young hands in Erin's gore. . . . .

[14] It may be felt that I have given Catherine too high a rank in my list. It is true that Byron treats her at length because she is necessary to the plot. However, I think that the emphasis she receives is not owing merely to the compulsion of the plot; Byron makes Catherine the grand epitome of despotism and hypocrisy.

[15] See Byron's "Preface" to Cantos VI, VII, and VIII (Oxford edition, p. 717). A concise account of the reasons for Byron's attitude toward Castlereagh is given by Prothero, *op. cit.*, IV, 108–9 n.

He accuses him of repairing Ireland's old fetters, and brands him (xiv) a "tinkering slave-maker," cobbling "manacles for all mankind." He is not a man, but a mere "*It*" which has (xv) "but two objects, how to serve, and bind." And "its" evil influence is felt not alone in England and Ireland but extends over Europe (xvi).

Another defect of Castlereagh's which arouses Byron's contempt (xiii) is his notorious deficiency in oratory:

> An orator of such set trash of phrase
> Ineffably—legitimately vile,
> That even its grossest flatterers dare not praise,
> Nor foes—all nations—condescend to smile;
> Not even a sprightly blunder's spark can blaze
> From that Ixion grindstone's ceaseless toil,
> That turns and turns to give the world a notion
> Of endless torments and perpetual motion.

With Byron the name Castlereagh is a byword for slovenly and careless rhetoric. Among his several sarcasms about Castlereagh's rhetoric are those in Cantos V (clxiii), VII (xvi), IX (xlix), and that (IX, l) in which Byron heaps up the derogatory epithets:

> I think I can explain myself without
> That sad inexplicable beast of prey—
> That Sphinx, whose words would ever be a doubt,
> Did not his deeds unriddle them each day—
> That monstrous hieroglyphic—that long spout
> Of blood and water, leaden Castlereagh!

Castlereagh's name is for Byron a synonym also for "taxes." In Canto II (cciii) Byron expresses the wonder that Castlereagh doesn't tax even "good old maxims," since it is his habit to tax everything that is good and pleasant. Again, in Canto VIII (cxxv) Byron suggests that

Castlereagh's name is inseparably linked with "Taxes" and "Debt."

A major portion of Byron's "Preface" to Cantos VI, VII, and VIII, of *Don Juan* is devoted to a virulent attack on Castlereagh:

As a minister, I, for one of millions, looked upon him as the most despotic in intention, and the weakest in intellect, that ever tyrannised over a country. It is the first time indeed since the Normans that England has been insulted by a *minister* (at least) who could not speak English, and that parliament permitted itself to be dictated to in the language of Mrs. Malaprop. . . . . In his death [suicide] he was necessarily one of two things by the *law*—a felon or a madman—and in either case no great subject for panegyric. In his life he was—what all the world knows, and half of it will feel for years to come, unless his death prove a "moral lesson" to the surviving Sejani of Europe. It may at least serve as some consolation to the nations, that their oppressors are not happy, and in some instances judge so justly of their own actions as to anticipate the sentence of mankind.—Let us hear no more of this man; and let Ireland remove the ashes of her Grattan from the sanctuary of Westminster. Shall the patriot of humanity repose by the Werther of politics!!![16]

Byron's last thrust at Castlereagh is in one of the *ubi sunt* stanzas in which he asks the rhetorical question, "Where little Castlereagh?" and answers, "The devil can tell" (XI, lxxvii).

Wordsworth also receives Byron's attention. Byron's quarrel with his fellow-poet is succinctly stated in his note to stanza vi of the "Dedication":

"And Wordsworth has his place in the Excise." Wordsworth's place may be in the Customs—it is, I think, in that or the Excise—besides another at Lord Lonsdale's table, where this poetical charlatan and political parasite licks up the crumbs with a hardened

[16] Byron's *Poetical Works*, p. 717.

alacrity; the converted Jacobin having long subsided into the clownish sycophant of the worst prejudices of the aristocracy.[17]

Byron's chief quarrel with Wordsworth, as is evident in this note, was what he regarded as Wordsworth's defection from political liberalism. Wordsworth had been an ardent liberal in the heady days of the French Revolution; but, like Southey, he subsequently relapsed into astute and orthodox conservatism. This apparent apostasy elicited Byron's contempt and scorn. Wordsworth's genuine poetic ability Byron did not for a moment seriously deny. He not only praised Wordsworth at times but even, upon occasion, wrote in the Wordsworthian manner and mood.[18] But, in general, Wordsworth's political conservatism and his "theory" of poetry were most distasteful to Byron.[19]

Wordsworth shares with Coleridge and Southey Byron's contemptuous appellation "Lakers." He accuses them of provincialism, of self-satisfaction, of selling themselves for money ("Dedication," v-vi).

In Canto I (xc–xci) Byron ridicules Wordsworth's obscurity at the same time that he satirizes his communion with nature, giving us what amounts almost to a parody of certain familiar passages of Wordsworth:

> Young Juan wander'd by the glassy brooks,
>   Thinking unutterable things; he threw
> Himself at length within the leafy nooks
>   Where the wild branch of the cork forest grew;
> There poets find materials for their books,
>   And every now and then we read them through,
> So that their plan and prosody are eligible,
> Unless, like Wordsworth, they prove unintelligible.

[17] Byron's *Poetical Works*, p. 894.

[18] See *Childe Harold*, Canto III, stanzas lxxii–lxxv.

[19] See Byron's *English Bards and Scotch Reviewers* (1809), in Byron's *Poetical Works*, pp. 114 and 122.

He, Juan (and not Wordsworth), so pursued
  His self-communion with his own high soul,
Until his mighty heart, in its great mood,
  Had mitigated part, though not the whole
Of its disease; he did the best he could
  With things not very subject to control,
And turn'd, without perceiving his condition,
Like Coleridge, into a metaphysician.

And, again, in the concluding stanza of Canto I (ccxxii),
Byron emphasizes Wordsworth's unintelligibility by saying
that he "can't help" putting in his own modest "claim to
praise" when "Southey's read, and Wordsworth understood."

Upon several occasions Byron expresses his annoyance
with Wordsworth's garrulous and didactic *Excursion*. The
first allusion to it is in the "Dedication," stanza iv:

And Wordsworth, in a rather long "Excursion"
  (I think the quarto holds five hundred pages),
Has given a sample from the vasty version
  Of his new system to perplex the sages;
'Tis poetry—at least by his assertion,
  And may appear so when the dog-star rages—
And he who understands it would be able
To add a story to the Tower of Babel.

He recurs to this theme in Canto III (xciv), again ex-
pressing his disgust with Wordsworth's

        drowsy frowzy poem, call'd the "Excursion,"
Writ in a manner which is my aversion.

He then (III, xcviii–c) pokes fun at Wordsworth's
"Waggoners," his "Pedlars," and his "Peter Bell," label-
ing them "trash," "bathos," and "drivel," and concluding
with a dramatic appeal to the shades of Pope and Dryden
who must endure the sneers of these "Jack Cades of sense
and song."

In Canto IV (cix), when he is referring jocosely to his own fancied decline from popular favor as a poet, Byron threatens to

> swear, as poet Wordy swore
> (Because the world won't read him, always snarling),
> That taste is gone, that fame is but a lottery,
> Drawn by the blue-coat misses of a coterie.

Wordsworth's apostasy from liberalism is a theme which Byron returns to with relish. He recalls (III, xciii) the former time when Wordsworth, "unexcised, unhired,"

> Season'd his pedlar poems with democracy;

but that time has long since vanished.

The last satiric reference to Wordsworth in *Don Juan* is Byron's biting irony with regard to one of Wordsworth's worst lapses. In the initial edition of Wordsworth's "Thanksgiving Ode" had occurred these lines:

> But Thy most dreaded instrument
> In working out a pure intent,
> Is man array'd for mutual slaughter;
> Yea, Carnage is thy daughter!

It was this genealogy of Carnage, omitted by Wordsworth from the later editions of his poems, which prompted Byron's allusion in his description (VIII, ix) of the Siege of Ismail:

> The columns were in movement one and all
>   But of the portion which attack'd by water,
> Thicker than leaves the lives began to fall,
>   Though led by Arseniew, that great son of slaughter,
> As brave as ever faced both bomb and ball.
>   "Carnage, (so Wordsworth tells you) is God's
>   daughter:"
> If *he* speaks truth, she is Christ's sister, and
> Just now behaved as in the Holy Land.

Byron gives a note on this line, "Carnage, (so Words-worth tells you) is God's daughter," in which he quotes the four lines from Wordsworth which I have cited. Re-ferring to the word "Thy" in the first of these lines, he says:

To wit, the Deity's; this is perhaps as pretty a pedigree for murder as ever was found out by Garter King at Arms.—What would they have said, had any free-spoken people discovered such a lineage?[20]

And, having disposed of Wordsworth, Byron plays the searching beam of his satire on the Duke of Wellington. Byron told the Countess of Blessington that it was the exaggerated praise of the people of England that "indis-posed" him to the Duke of Wellington. Byron well knew the fickleness of English approval:

I know that the same herd, who were trying to make an idol of him, would, on any reverse, or change of opinions, hurl him from the pedestal to which they had raised him, and lay their idol in the dust.[21]

But Byron's chief motive was his contempt for the Duke as a national leader who had forfeited all claim to the gratitude of the common people by allying himself with their oppressors.[22]

Byron also despised Wellington as the embodiment of the war spirit. He devotes the first ten stanzas of Canto IX to a spirited satire of Wellington as the personification of this spirit. After posing as the defender and liberator of the people of Europe, Wellington has, in reality, "re-

[20] See Byron's *Poetical Works*, p. 899.

[21] Blessington, *op. cit.*, p. 360.

[22] That is, by countenancing and supporting the Holy Alliance. For Byron's attitude toward Wellington and the Holy Alliance, see the introduction to *The Age of Bronze* in the Coleridge edition of Byron's *Works*, V, 537–40.

paired Legitimacy's crutch" and restored tyranny in Spain,
France, and Holland. Who, asks Byron (IX, v), except
Wellington, "the best of cut-throats," has gained by Waterloo? He has been flattered and eulogized "for every
lucky blunder" by the speakers in Parliament and has been
called

> "Saviour of the Nations"—not yet saved,
> And "Europe's Liberator"—still enslaved.

He dines in sumptuous luxury while England goes
hungry. Unlike other "great men," he expects and accepts
remuneration for his achievements (IX, vi–x).

"Never had mortal man such opportunity," says Byron,
"or abused it more." He might have been Europe's de-
liverer from tyranny; instead (IX, ix), what *is* his fame?

> Go! hear it in your famish'd country's cries!
> Behold the world! and curse your victories!

He continues (IX, x):

> As these new cantos touch on warlike feats,
>   To *you* the unflattering Muse deigns to inscribe
> Truths, that you will not read in the Gazettes,
>   But which 'tis time to teach the hireling tribe
> Who fatten on their country's gore, and debts
>   Must be recited—and without a bribe.
> You *did great* things: but not being *great* in mind,
> Have left *undone* the *greatest*—and mankind.

Byron even dares to suggest (VIII, xlviii–xlix) that
Wellington might have been defeated at Waterloo, and
might not now be receiving "pensions, which are the heav-
iest that our history mentions," had it not been for the
assistance of Blücher, Bülow, Gneisenau, and others.
Among other sarcasms about Wellington are these: Byron
remarks (VIII, ccxv) that the English and Irish go hungry
while their hunger is fed only with "Wellesley's glory";

and in Canto XII (xx) Byron contrasts Wilberforce who "set free the Negroes" with the Duke of Wellington who "has but enslaved the Whites."

The major details of the notorious "Separation" of Lord and Lady Byron are too well known to require any setting-forth here. The whole complex problem of the relations between Byron and his wife, which, obviously enough, is quite outside the scope of this study, is clearly and adequately stated in the biographies of Lord and Lady Byron by Ethel C. Mayne.[23]

The character of Donna Inez, Juan's mother, as it is drawn by Byron in Canto I, stanzas x–xxx, is a very obvious parallel of the character and manners of Lady Byron. It was these stanzas which were denounced in *Blackwood's* for August 1819 as "an elaborate satire on the character and manners of his wife."

Byron emphasizes the parallel by remarking Donna Inez's mathematical ability and her erudition in general (I, x–xiv), her incomparable virtues (I, xvii), her impeccable moral character (I, xvi), and her self-righteousness (I, xx). She is a "walking calculation" and "Morality's prim personification." To clinch the parallel, Byron has Donna Inez and her husband, Don José, quarrel (I, xxiii), and afterward (xxvii) Donna Inez attempts to "prove her loving lord was *mad*." Failing in this, Donna Inez records her husband's faults in a journal, adds to these the findings of a surreptitious search through his letters, and repeats the sum total of her husband's crimes to the "hearers of her case," who, in turn, become (xxviii) repeaters,

> Then advocates, inquisitors, and judges,
> Some for amusement, others for old grudges.

[23] Ethel C. Mayne, *Byron* (London, 1924), and *The Life and Letters of Anne Isabella, Lady Noel Byron* (New York, 1929).

Finally (I, xxix), when the cries of calumny arose against her husband, she

> saw *his* agonies with such sublimity,
> That all the world exclaim'd, "What magnanimity!"

It is also quite likely that Byron was thinking of his wife when, in his "poetical commandments," he said (I, ccvi):

> Thou shalt not bear false witness like "the Blues"—
> (There's one, at least, is very fond of this).

Again, he alludes to Lady Byron, and to the calumny which fastened upon him the moment his wife left him, when he speaks (III, xxxiv)

> Of magic ladies who, by one sole act,
> Transformed their lords to beasts (but that's a fact).

In Canto VIII Byron, in describing the grim uncertainty of war, compares (xxvii) the "strange chance" which separates warriors in battle to the stranger chance which leads

> chastest wives from constant husbands' sides
> Just at the close of the first bridal year.

Byron's accusation of his wife is very thinly disguised in this stanza (XIV, xcv):

> Alas! by all experience, seldom yet
> (I merely quote what I have heard from many)
> Had lovers not some reason to regret
> The passion which made Solomon a zany.
> I've also seen some wives (not to forget
> The marriage state, the best or worst of any)
> Who were the very paragons of wives,
> Yet made the misery of at least two lives.

His last satiric allusion to Lady Byron in *Don Juan* is in Canto XV (xli), where in the description of Miss Millpond, one of Lady Adeline's house-guests, he epitomizes the character of his wife:

There was Miss Millpond, smooth as summer's sea,
  That usual paragon, an only daughter,
Who seem'd the cream of equanimity,
  Till skimm'd—and then there was some milk and water,
With a light shade of blue too, it might be
  Beneath the surface; but what did it matter?
Love's riotous, but marriage should have quiet,
And being consumptive, live on a milk diet.

Prince George succeeded his demented father as King of England by the authority of the Regency Bill, which was passed on February 5, 1810. It was generally supposed that, as King, the Regent would recompense the Whigs who, throughout his many difficulties, had so faithfully supported him. But general expectation was unrealized; for George IV, failing in an effort to organize a coalition ministry, appointed Lord Liverpool as Prime Minister and thus the Tories retained the domination of the affairs of state. The Whigs, regarding this as treachery, were irreconcilable and never ceased reviling the King who had broken faith with them.[24] Byron was one of the political liberals who never became reconciled to the King. While his most bitter denunciation of George IV is in "The Irish Avatar" (1821), his *Don Juan* contains a number of taunts and sarcasms directed at the King.

Byron's first thrust is his ironic suggestion (VIII, cxxvi) that the starving Irish have one sublime consolation, namely, the knowledge that

Howe'er the mighty locust, Desolation
  Strip your green fields, and to your harvest cling,
Gaunt famine never shall approach the throne—
Though Ireland starve, great **George** weighs **twenty**
  stone.

[24] See Byron's "Lines to a Lady Weeping" (1812), addressed to Princess Charlotte, daughter of the Prince Regent.

In Canto IX (xxxviii–xl) Byron classes George IV with other "relics" which, when the aeons have passed, will be dug up and regarded as "monsters of a new museum."

The other sarcasms about George IV in *Don Juan* are these: In the *ubi sunt* stanzas Byron says (XI, lxxxiii) he has seen the King hissed and then caressed, "But don't pretend to settle which was best." He is undoubtedly thinking of King George as one of the kings to whom he refers when he says (XI, lxxxiv), "I have seen crowns worn instead of a fool's cap." There is another slur about "these times of low taxation" (XVI, lvi) and a final jibe (XVI, lxxiv) about

> The Gordian or the Geordi-an knot, whose strings
> Have tied together commons, lords, and kings.

Samuel Taylor Coleridge's abstruse and metaphysical tendencies, in his poetry as well as in his prose, annoyed Byron, as well as the fact that he, like Wordsworth, had abandoned the political liberalism of his younger years.[25] In the "Dedication" (ii) of *Don Juan* Byron ridicules Coleridge as another of the "Lakers," who has "lately taken wing,"

> Explaining metaphysics to the nation—
> I wish he would explain his Explanation.

Coleridge shares with Wordsworth Byron's banter about communion with nature. The lovelorn Juan, in his solitary sylvan wanderings, turns (I, xci)

> without perceiving his condition,
> Like Coleridge, into a metaphysician.

[25] For Byron's earlier satire of Coleridge in *English Bards and Scotch Reviewers* see Byron's *Poetical Works*, p. 114.

Again, Byron derides Coleridge's didacticism and jokes about his having, like Southey, espoused "Pantisocracy" as well as two "milliners of Bath." A variant reading for the sixth line in this stanza reads "Flourished its sophistry for aristocracy"—suggesting that Coleridge, like Wordsworth, from being a democrat has become a flatterer of aristocracy.

Of the second group of individuals, composed of those who receive satiric mention in *Don Juan* less frequently than those so far dealt with, Lord Brougham is prominent. Seven stanzas which Byron wrote on Lord Brougham, to be inserted in Canto I after stanza clxxxix, he had Murray withhold and they were first printed in the Coleridge edition of *Don Juan*.[26] Another probable reference to Brougham is in the description of the guests at Lord and Lady Amundeville's house party in Canto XIII (lxxxiv); Coleridge is of the opinion that Byron intended "Parolles," "the legal bully," for Lord Brougham.[27]

It was undoubtedly Lady Caroline Lamb, who plagued Byron with her attentions during the heyday of his London popularity, whom he has in mind in the concluding line of his epitome of womankind in Canto II, stanza cci; he alludes to the novel which she had written and in which he himself had figured, in the line "Some play the devil, and then write a novel."[28] He alludes to her again in the *ubi sunt* stanzas (XI, lxxx):

> Where are the Lady Carolines and Franceses?
> Divorced or doing thereanent.

Joanna Southcote, a demented poetess who thought she was another Virgin Mary, drew Byron's scorn in this stanza (III, xcv):

[26] See Coleridge edition of Byron's *Poetical Works*, VI, 67 ff.
[27] *Ibid.*, VI, 506.
[28] The novel was *Glenarvon* (1817).

But Wordsworth's poem, and his followers, like
Joanna Southcote's Shiloh, and her sect,
Are things which in this century don't strike
The public mind,—so few are the elect;
And the new births of both their stale virginities
Have proved but dropsies, taken for divinities.

And in the "I have seen" stanzas (XI, lxxxiv) he refers
to her again as one of the curiosities of his time.

The Russian marshal, Suwarrow, Byron disparages for
his military ruthlessness and callousness to human suffering. He was a "match for Timour or for Zinghis" in
cruelty, and "could rhyme like Nero, o'er a burning city"
(VIII, cxxxiii–cxxxiv). Suwarrow's callousness is further
emphasized by Byron in Canto IX (lx), where he speaks
of the shudder which runs naturally through our veins
when "things call'd sovereigns think it best to kill, and
generals turn it into jest."

Napoleon's retreat from Moscow is alluded to in a
stanza (X, lviii) in which Byron calls him the "modern
Mars." Again, he speaks contemptuously of the overthrow
of Napoleon,[29] saying (XI, lxxxiii):

I have seen Napoleon, who seem'd quite a Jupiter,
    Shrink to a Saturn.

Byron makes several ironic allusions to Malthus. He
promises to be as serious in Canto XII as if he had Malthus
and Wilberforce for his inditers. But while he praises
Wilberforce, he asserts that Malthus doesn't practice what
he preaches. Byron is very likely referring (XII, xx) to
the apocryphal story of Malthus' "eleven daughters."
And in the next stanza he speaks scornfully of sages who

---

[29] See also Byron's "Ode to Napoleon Buonaparte" (1814) in
Byron's *Poetical Works*, pp. 72–74.

write against all procreation,
Unless a man can calculate his means
Of feeding brats the moment his wife weans.

Byron again makes fun of the Malthusian marriage economics, suggesting (XV, xxxviii) that "it conducts to lives ascetic, or turning marriage into arithmetic."

In the considerable list of those to whom Byron makes at least one satiric reference in *Don Juan*, I shall merely mention each individual in turn, giving the textual reference, and noting what it is that elicits Byron's satire in each case.

The first of these is Mr. Sotheby whom Byron numbers with the untouchables in his "poetical commandments" (I, ccvi). Queen Caroline's amours with Bergami are hinted at in Canto VI; one of the advocates employed for Queen Caroline in the House of Lords had spoken of some of the most puzzling passages in the history of her intercourse with Bergami as amounting to "odd instances of strange coincidence"—hence Byron's allusion (VI, lxxviii) to "strange coincidence."[30] Byron's one satiric reference in *Don Juan* to his publisher, John Murray, is an allusion (VII, xxvi) to the haste and carelessness with which some of his cantos had been printed. Potemkin is most vigorously denounced (VII, xxxvi–xli) for his o'erweening self-pride and his ruthless military machinations. Another militarist despicable in Byron's sight is General Markow, who, during the Siege of Ismail, is zealous to rescue wounded "princes" but has no time for "common fellows who might writhe and wince" (VIII, xi). William Pitt, in contrast to Wellington, illustrates how "great men" scorn "great recompenses," in that *he* ruined Britain "gratis" (IX, viii). Queen Elizabeth, "our own half-chaste Elizabeth," is accused (IX, lxxxi) of moral hypocrisy and ava-

---

[30] See Coleridge, *op. cit.*, VI, 290.

rice. The poetry of the Reverend George Croly, D.D. (1780–1860), dramatic critic, novelist, and preacher, is disparaged (XI, lvii) by Byron as having a "psalmodic amble." Henry Hart Milman is apparently the individual referred to by Byron in Canto XI, stanza lviii, which was first published[31] in 1837; Byron, under the impression that Milman had influenced Murray against continuing the publication of *Don Juan,* calls him (XI, lviii) "that ox of verse" because he had recently been appointed Professor of Poetry at Oxford. Byron speaks sarcastically (XI, lix) of Bryan Waller Proctor (Barry Cornwall) "as a sort of *moral me.*" Jeffrey had compared Cornwall's "Diego de Montilla," a poem in *ottava rima,* with Byron's *Don Juan* to the disadvantage of the latter, and also had praised Cornwall's poem for its superior virtue. There is both praise and belittlement of John Keats in stanza lx of Canto XI. Brummell and Whitbread are named among those who have vanished from this world rather ungracefully— by suicide (XI, lxxviii). Lady Frances Wedderburn Webster, like Lady Caroline Lamb, is "divorced or doing thereanent" (XI, lxxx). William Mitford draws Byron's disapproval (XII, xix) for having abused Plutarch and praised tyrants in his history of Greece. Lord Eldon, who in February 1822 had refused the motion for an injunction to restrain the defendant from publishing a pirated edition of Byron's *Cain,* received brief mention from Byron in connection with his remarks on chancery (XII, xviii). According to E. H. Coleridge, there was an erased stanza in Canto XII, following stanza xviii, which satirized Lord Eldon.[32] Izaak Walton, the patron saint of anglers, receives short shrift from Byron as a "quaint, old, cruel coxcomb" who should have tried being on the other end of a fishing line (XIII, cvi). The "Peter Pith" of the Nor-

[31] Coleridge, *op. cit.,* VI, 445.
[32] *Ibid.,* VI, 460, note 1.

man Abbey house party is Sidney Smith;[33] "His jokes," says Byron, "were sermons and his sermons jokes" (XVI, lxxxi–lxxxiii). Finally, Sir William Curtis Byron calls "a bore, too dull even for the dullest of excesses" and "the witless Falstaff of a hoary Hal" (X, lxxxvi).

According to E. H. Coleridge, only a few of the shadowy members of the Norman Abbey house party can be materialized.[34] Those few are: "Dick Dubious," the metaphysician who loved philosophy and a good dinner (XIII, lxxxvii), who Coleridge thinks may be James Mackintosh; "General Fireface," who "ate" in the last war more Yankees than he "kill'd" (XIII, lxxxviii), who Coleridge is certain is intended for Sir George Prevost, the Governor-General of British North America and nominally Commander-in-Chief of the Army in the second American War, who contributed, by his excessive caution and delay, to the humiliation of the British forces; "Longbow" and "Strongbow" (XIII, xcii–xciii) who Coleridge is positive are to be identified with John Philpot Curran and Thomas Lord Erskine; and "Kit-Cat," the famous "Conversationalist," who "prepared" and "studied" his "bons-mots" (XIII, xcvii), who Coleridge thinks may be Richard Sharp, known in society as "Conversation Sharp."

Now let us survey the collection of individuals whom Byron satirizes to see if there is any consistency in his choice. With a few exceptions they are rulers, statesmen, politicians, and literary men. A small group of about five Byron satirizes for purely personal reasons. The rest are a miscellaneous group pilloried for their respective idiosyncrasies and hypocrisies. And in Byron's satire of individuals several rather clearly defined objectives can be distinguished. Thus:

---

[33] *Ibid.*, VI, 596 f. Smith's "Letters of Peter Plymley" may have suggested the name.

[34] *Ibid.*, VI, 504.

Satire of Tyranny and Oppression:

Catherine of Russia   Lord Brougham
Viscount Castlereagh   William Pitt
King George IV   William Mitford

Satire of Militarism:

The Duke of Wellington   Napoleon
Marshal Suwarrow   Catherine of Russia
Prince Potemkin   General Markow

Satire of Political Opportunism and Reactionary Conservatism:

Robert Southey   Samuel Taylor Coleridge
William Wordsworth   Rev. T. R. Malthus

Satire of Moral Hypocrisy:

Catherine of Russia   Queen Elizabeth
                    Queen Caroline

Satire of Literary Idiosyncrasy:

Samuel Taylor Coleridge   Barry Cornwall
William Wordsworth   John Keats
Joanna Southcote   Rev. George Croly
Henry Hart Milman   William Sotheby

Satire Motivated by Personal Grievance:

Lady Byron   Lady Caroline Lamb
Robert Southey   Lord Eldon
Lady Frances Wedderburn Webster John Murray

Satire of Miscellaneous Hypocrisies and Idiosyncrasies:

Izaak Walton   Sir Samuel Romilly
Sidney Smith   Beau Brummell
Sir William Curtis   Samuel Whitbread

The five identified members of the Norman Abbey house party

A comparison of these classified lists of individuals with the original lists, in which the names are arranged according to the amount of attention they receive from Byron, reveals that Byron's major objectives, or emphases, in his satire of individuals are tyranny and oppression, militarism, political conservatism, and moral hypocrisy. The eight individuals to whom Byron devotes the greater part of his satiric attention are, with the possible exception of Lady Byron, persons whom Byron associates with these defects in society. As for the rest of the individuals whom Byron satirizes, clearly their actual or alleged affectations and hypocrisies are responsible for his ridicule.[35] With the exception of the satire of literary foibles and the satire motivated by personal grievance, Byron's satire of individuals has, then, two major objectives: the ridicule of all insincerity and the denunciation of all that obstructs individual and national freedom.

III

SATIRE OF ENGLAND AND THINGS ENGLISH

Byron's condemnation of England and things English is severe and thoroughgoing. He inveighs against the manifold abuses in English government, politics, and economy. He ridicules the much-vaunted English freedom and morality. He satirizes English clergy, poets,

[35] Byron probably was acquainted with Fielding's theory of the "Ridiculous" as it appears in *Joseph Andrews*. "The only source of the true Ridiculous (as it appears to me) is affectation. . . . . Now, affectation proceeds from one of these two causes, vanity or hypocrisy: for as vanity puts us on affecting false characters, in order to purchase applause; so hypocrisy sets us on an endeavour to avoid censure by concealing our vices under an appearance of their opposite virtues." See Fielding's preface to *Joseph Andrews*, Everyman edition, p. xl.

lawyers, doctors, statesmen, "placemen," and country gentlemen, and derides the hypocrisy of English "high society." As we shall see, the predominant motive behind
his satire of England and things English is detestation of
insincerity and oppression.

Let us first observe his satire of English government
and national policy. Debt, taxes, famine, and the sufferings of Ireland under English misrule are the themes on
which Byron again and again rings the changes. John Bull,
declares Byron (VII, xlv), must be blind since he calls
debt "wealth," taxes "Paradise," and ignores "Famine."
If Byron wishes an illustration of the evils of govern-
mental mismanagement he turns to English taxes, debt,
and oppression of the Irish (VIII, cxxv–cxxvi). In the
ubi sunt stanzas he calls the House of Commons a "tax-
trap" (XI, lxxxiv); and in Canto XII (lxvii) he reiterates
the charge of over-taxation when he speaks of England as

> the shore
> Of white cliffs, white necks, blue eyes, bluer stockings,
> Tithes, taxes, duns, and doors with double knockings.

Mismanagement, corruption, and oppression are the
abuses in English government which he repeatedly denounces (e.g., XI, lxxxv). He singles out the Chancellors
of the Exchequer for censure, declaring (XVI, xcix):

> The poets of arithmetic are they
>   Who, though they prove not two and two to be
> Five, as they might do in a modest way,
>   Have plainly made it out that four are three,
> Judging by what they take, and what they pay.
>   The Sinking Fund's unfathomable sea,
> That most unliquidating liquid, leaves
> The debt unsunk, yet sinks all it receives.

He derides the inefficiency of the English Parliament
in a stanza (XIII, xxix) which ironically suggests that

"Britain's present wealth and happiness" must be owing to the "collective wisdom" of the "senate." And while he is hymning the praises of the English Parliament, Byron hastens to give that august body credit for another of its important functions—that of serving as a "barometer" or almanac of the otherwise hopelessly confused and ambiguous English seasons (XIII, xliii).

Byron turns his attention next to English character. He contrasts (XI, xliv) English "downright rudeness" with French "true or false politeness." The English, he goes on to say, are not a people free from vices, but their vices are the fruit of mature and careful deliberation. He continues (XI, lxxi):

> impatience is a blundering guide,
> Amongst a people famous for reflection,
> Who like to play the fool with circumspection.

The English, he says (XII, lxv), are zealous to avoid the appearance of evil but have a decided taste for lawsuits and a relish for scandal:

> For 'tis a low, newspaper, humdrum, lawsuit
>   Country, where a young couple of the same ages
> Can't form a friendship, but the world o'er-awes it.
>   Then there's the vulgar trick of those d——d damages!
> A verdict—grievous foe to those who cause it!—
>   Forms a sad climax to romantic homages;
> Besides those soothing speeches of the pleaders,
> And evidences which regale all readers.

The Englishman is a rather passionless sort of fellow who has a number of interests which absorb his attention and take the place of passions, love, and other hallucinations. Parliament, religion, reform, peace, war, taxes, debt, and "the joys of mutual hate" (XIII, v–vi) are adequate compensation. "Ennui," he suggests (XIII, ci), "is a growth of English root." Continuing in the same vein, Byron

satirizes the English lack of emotion and *finesse* in the art
of love. He takes Lord Henry Amundeville as typical of
the English phlegmatic character (XIV, lxx–lxxi):

> He was a cold, good, honourable man,
>   Proud of his birth, and proud of everything;
> A goodly spirit for a state divan,
>   A figure fit to walk before a king;
> Tall, stately, form'd to lead the courtly van
>   On birthdays, glorious with a star and string;
> The very model of a chamberlain—
> And such I mean to make him when I reign.
>
> But there was something wanting on the whole—
>   I don't know what, and therefore cannot tell—
> Which pretty women—the sweet souls!—call *soul*.
>   *Certes* it was not body; he was well
> Proportion'd, as a poplar or a pole,
>   A handsome man, that human miracle;·
> And in each circumstance of love or war
> Had still preserved his perpendicular.

The much-vaunted English "freedom" next (X, lxvi–
lxviii) draws Byron's scorn:

> I've no great cause to love that spot of earth,
>   Which holds what *might have been* the noblest nation;
> But though I owe it little but my birth,
>   I feel a mix'd regret and veneration
> For its decaying fame and former worth.
>   Seven years (the usual term of transportation)
> Of absence lay one's old resentments level,
> When a man's country's going to the devil.
>
> Alas! could she but fully, truly know
>   How her great name is now throughout abhorr'd;
> How eager all the earth is for the blow
>   Which shall lay bare her bosom to the sword;

How all the nations deem her their worst foe,
  That worse than *worst of foes*, the once adored
False friend, who held out freedom to mankind,
And now would chain them, to the very mind;—

Would she be proud, or boast herself the free,
  Who is but first of slaves? The nations are
In prison,—but the gaoler, what is he?
  No less a victim to the bolt and bar.
Is the poor privilege to turn the key
  Upon the captive, freedom? He's as far
From the enjoyment of the earth and air
Who watches o'er the chain, as they who wear.

But in enchaining freedom elsewhere in Europe England is but putting herself to prison. And England's "free millions" have learned not to "kick against the pricks" lest they get "only a fresh puncture" for their pains (X, lxxvii). A few stanzas farther on (X, lxxxi) Byron charges England with having "butchered" half the earth and "bullied" the other half, referring, no doubt, to India and America.

Byron's irony is nowhere more effective than in the Shooter's Hill episode, where Juan, rapt in contemplation of London Town, ponders on English "freedom." His reverential mood is rudely interrupted (XI, viii–xi) by the pressure of a knife at his back and the "freeborn sounds"—"Damn your eyes! your money or your life!"

With increasing earnestness Byron turns from the satire of English "freedom" to the satire of English "morality." He refuses (XI, lxxxvii) to join in the popular cant about England's superior morality:

But how shall I relate in other cantos
  Of what befell our hero in the land
Which 'tis the common cry and lie to vaunt as
  A moral country? But I hold my hand—

> For I disdain to write an Atalantis;
> But 'tis as well at once to understand
> You are *not* a moral people, and you know it
> Without the aid of too sincere a poet.

Not only does he refuse to join in the "common cry and lie" but sets about (XI, lxxxvii) to demonstrate its falsity. He begins (XI, xii) with the ridicule of English profanity. He next makes (XI, xv) an odious comparison between "innkeepers" and "highwaymen." After this he advises (XI, lxxxvi) his hero, newly arrived in England, to be "hypocritical" if he would be well received by the English:

> . . . . keep a sharp eye
> Much less on what you do than what you say:
> Be hypocritical, be cautious, be
> Not what you *seem*, but always what you *see*.

For it is *"tact"* that saves the day in England—*"tact,"* the *sine qua non* of English virtue and respectability (XII, lxvi). On the Continent passion has something of the "frantic"; but in England it is "half commercial, half pedantic" and "half a fashion" (XII, lxviii). On the Continent a lapse from strictest virtue is forgivable; not so in "moral" England (XII, lxxviii):

> The reason's obvious: if there's an eclat,
>   They lose their caste at once, as do the Parias;
> And when the delicacies of the law
>   Have fill'd their papers with their comments various,
> Society, that china without flaw,
>   (The hypocrite!) will banish them like Marius,
> To sit amidst the ruins of their guilt:
> For Fame's a Carthage not so soon rebuilt.

According to Canto XII, stanzas lxxix–lxxx, there is no forgiving, "Christian" spirit among English society. Abroad, "an erring woman finds an opener door for her return to Virtue." The harsh English treatment of lapses from virtue leads to false morality and to caring more for "discoveries" than "deeds." Chastity is not to be bound by laws which but aggravate the crime they are helpless to prevent.

If one would attain worldly success in this "moral nation" he must become an opportunist, says Byron (XIII, xviii), and learn to discipline his conscience.

Not for a moment is Byron lenient with English moral hypocrisy. One of his last flings in *Don Juan* at the cant of "propriety" is the following (XVI, lii):

> But so far the immediate effect
>   Was to restore him to his self-propriety,
> A thing quite necessary to the elect,
>   Who wish to take the tone of their society:
> In which you cannot be too circumspect,
>   Whether the mode be persiflage or piety,
> But wear the newest mantle of hypocrisy,
> On pain of much displeasing the gynocracy.

English "high society" draws Byron's ridicule. Pausing at the conclusion of his tenth canto (lxxxiv–lxxxvii), "as doth a crew before they give their broadside," he promises, if not threatens, to tell his countrymen truths they "will not take as true, because they are so." He will be a "male Mrs. Fry," only, instead of going to Newgate he will begin with Carlton House and other fashionable houses, with the idea of trying his hand at "harden'd and imperial sin" and making the people's "betters better."

Byron's subject is London "high society," England's socially elite, whom he characterizes very neatly in these four lines (XI, xlv):

> And about twice two thousand people bred
>   By no means to be very wise or witty,
> But to sit up while others lie in bed,
>   And look down on the universe with pity,—

The frivolous and superficial life of London's socially elite is faithfully represented in Canto XI, stanzas lxv–lxxii. The superficiality of their criteria of worth, their overemphasis of wealth and fashionable appearance, and their boundless conceit are grist for Byron's satiric mill (XII, xxviii). He ridicules the selfish conceit of the socially elite by referring to them (XIII, xlix) as:

The twice two thousand for whom earth was made—

And again (XII, lvi):

Don Juan saw that microcosm on stilts,
    Yclept the Great World; for it is the least,
Although the highest: but as swords have hilts
    By which their power of mischief is increased,
When man in battle or in quarrel tilts,
    Thus the low world, north, south, or west, or east,
Must still obey the high—which is their handle,
Their moon, their sun, their gas, their farthing candle.

In comparing English pastoral pastimes with Italian, Byron suggests (XIII, lxxviii) that, although England has no "wild boars,"

she hath a tame
Preserve of bores, who ought to be made game.

This "tame preserve of bores" Byron derides (XIII, lxxx) as at once the "lie" and the "*élite*" of crowds. If Byron meant "lee" by "lie," as E. H. Coleridge suggests,[36] his meaning is apparent. He is sneering at the hypocritical virtue of these people who are at once the froth and the dregs of society.

Juan, entering this little world of English high society, finds (XI, xlv) that he, as a "patrician," is "well received by persons of condition." Fair virgins and wedded dames, both of which "commodities" dwell by the Thames,

[36] Coleridge, *op. cit.*, VI, 505.

"blush'd upon him," and "pious mothers inquired his income" (XI, xlviii). In fact, Juan finds himself (XII, xxxii–xxxvi) not only a spectator but an unwilling participant in the London marriage mart with its sophistry, gossip, backbiting, bargaining, perjury, and pronounced commercial character.

Escaping unscathed from the clutches of virgins, mothers, and married dames, Juan finds himself (XIII, lxxxv, lxxxvi) a house guest of Lord Henry Amundeville, a typical male example of English social aristocracy. Among the fashionable people assembled at Lord Henry's country place were twelve peers,

> and all such peers in look
> And intellect, that neither eyes nor ears
> For commoners had ever them mistook.

And, also, there were

> four Honourable Misters, whose
> Honour was more before their names than after;

After comparing the "good company" to chessmen and puppets, Byron ridicules (XIII, xciv, xcv) their monotonous and slavish conformity to convention:

> If all these seem a heterogeneous mass
>   To be assembled at a country seat,
> Yet think, a specimen of every class
>   Is better than a humdrum tete-a-tete.
> The days of Comedy are gone, alas!
>   When Congreve's fool could vie with Molière's *bête:*
> Society is smooth'd to that excess,
> That manners hardly differ more than dress.
>
> Our ridicules are kept in the back ground—
>   Ridiculous enough, but also dull;
> Professions, too, are no more to be found
>   Professional; and there is nought to cull

Of folly's fruit; for though your fools abound,
 They're barren, and not worth the pains to pull.
Society is now one polish'd horde,
Form'd of two mighty tribes, the *Bores* and *Bored*.

Byron contrasts (XIII, cx) the lukewarmness and in-
sipidity of manners of the high society of his day with the
gusto of a former day:

But all was gentle and aristocratic
 In this our party; polish'd, smooth, and cold,
As Phidian forms cut out of marble Attic.
 There now are no Squire Westerns as of old;
And our Sophias are not so emphatic,
 But fair as then, or fairer to behold.
We have no accomplish'd blackguards, like Tom Jones,
But gentlemen in stays, as stiff as stones.

Near the beginning of Canto XIV Byron comments on
the "beau monde," the theme of his "following sermon,"
and suggests (XIV, xv–xvii) that it is a portion of the
world that is not frequently described by writers because
of its dull, humdrum, commonplace, and monotonous nature. All poets who have endeavored to paint "the *real*
portrait of the highest tribe" have failed miserably because "there's little to describe" (xx). In short, the *beau
monde* is a "paradise of pleasure and ennui" (xvii).

In the ensuing brilliant lines (xviii) Byron epitomizes
the round of life in such circles:

When we have made our love, and gamed our gaming,
 Drest, voted, shone, and, may be, something more;
With dandies dined; heard senators declaiming;
 Seen beauties brought to market by the score,
Sad rakes to sadder husbands chastely taming;
 There's little left but to be bored or bore.

Turning from his satire of English high society, Byron
attacks the clergy (VII, vi) with these words:

> Ecclesiastes said, "that all is vanity"—
> Most modern preachers say the same, or show it
> By their examples of true Christianity:

He makes another disparaging reference to them when (XVI, lxxx) he is listing the guests at Lord Henry's electioneering banquet:

> There were some massy members of the church,
> Takers of tithes, and makers of good matches,
> And several who sung fewer psalms than catches.

And he gives us a full-length portrait (XVI, lxxxi–lxxxiii) of one of these English parsons, "Peter Pith,"

> that o'erwhelming son of heaven,
> The very powerful parson, Peter Pith,
> The loudest wit I e'er was deafen'd with.

This was probably Sidney Smith, to whom Byron refers in *English Bards and Scotch Reviewers* as "Smug Sidney." In his London days Smith was a "brilliant diner out" and not a joke he told "but earn'd its praise." But preferment, that evidence of the wondrous benevolence of Providence, gave him a "fat fen vicarage and nought to think on" (lxxxii). And so, the poor priest's jokes, which "were sermons," and his sermons, which were "jokes," "both were thrown away amongst the fens" (lxxxiii).

The "recent poets" of Byron's day did not escape his disapproval. He says (II, cxxiv):

> I hate all mystery, and that air
> Of clap-trap, which your recent poets prize;

And, again, after praising some of the writers of English prose, he avows (II, clxv) his detestation of English poets: "I hate your poets, so read none of those."[37]

---

[37] Byron makes a jocular reference to Shakespeare (VII, xxi) and "his plays so doting" with the express purpose, I think, of annoying the English. His attitude toward the chief contemporary poets of his day we have already seen in his satire of individuals.

Byron's hero, initiated into the "coteries" of English high society, sees (XI, liv) the "ten thousand living authors" pass in review, as well as "the eighty 'greatest living poets'."

From English poets Byron's satire shifts to English lawyers. He was more than likely thinking of an English lawyer when he sketched the attorney in Julia's boudoir in Canto I (clx):

> With prying snub-nose, and small eyes, he stood,
>   Following Antonia's motions here and there,
> With much suspicion in his attitude;
>   For reputations he had little care;
> So that a suit or action were made good,
>   Small pity had he for the young and fair,
> And ne'er believed in negatives, till these
> Were proved by competent false witnesses.

We know from the context of the following stanzas (X, xiv, xv) that they were prompted by Byron's own unpleasant experiences with English lawyers:

> The lawyer and the critic but behold
>   The baser sides of literature and life,
> And naught remains unseen, but much untold,
>   By those who scour those double vales of strife.
> While common men grow ignorantly old,
>   The lawyer's brief is like the surgeon's knife,
> Dissecting the whole inside of a question,
> And with it all the process of digestion.
>
> A legal broom's a moral chimney-sweeper,
>   And that's the reason he himself's so dirty!
> The endless soot bestows a tint far deeper
>   Than can be hid by altering his shirt; he
> Retains the sable stains, of the dark creeper,
>   At least some twenty-nine do out of thirty,
> In all their habits;—

Byron further supplies (XIII, lxix) the critical anno-
tations for the portraits of English judges and attorneys-
general which hung in the gallery of Norman Abbey:

> Judges in very formidable ermine
>   Were there, with brows that did not much invite
> The accused to think their lordships would determine
>   His cause by leaning much from might to right:
> Bishops, who had not left a single sermon;
>   Attorneys-general, awful to the sight,
> As hinting more (unless our judgment warp us)
> Of the "Star Chamber" than of "Habeas Corpus."

Byron's contempt for English "placemen," clerks, pen-
sioners, politicians, and all the tribe of "underlings" expresses itself rather violently in these stanzas (XI, xli):

> Besides the ministers and underlings,
>   Who must be courteous to the accredited
> Diplomatists of rather wavering kings,
>   Until their royal riddle's fully read,
> The very clerks,—those somewhat dirty springs
>   Of office, or the house of office, fed
> By foul corruption into streams,—even they
> Were hardly rude enough to earn their pay:
>
> And insolence no doubt is what they are
>   Employ'd for, since it is their daily labour,
> In the dear offices of peace or war;
>   And should you doubt, pray ask of your next neighbor,
> When for a passport, or some other bar
>   To freedom, he applied (a grief and a bore),
> If he found not in this spawn of taxborn riches,
> Like lap-dogs, the least civil sons of b——s.

Throughout Cantos XIII, XIV, and XV there are
many stanzas of banter about the artificiality of English
country life and an extended description of the members
of the Norman Abbey house party. In Canto XVI Byron

gives us, in his description of Lord Henry Amundeville, a satirical portrait of a typical English country gentleman. Lord Henry is a connoisseur of art who prides himself upon his judgment, "never known to fail" (XVI, lvii). One important evidence of his taste is his "restoration" of an ancient Gothic abbey which he had acquired (lviii–lix). Lord Henry maintains two lawyers who are "busy on a mortgage Lord Henry wish'd to raise for a new purchase" (lx). Being a justice of the peace, he must deal out justice to "two poachers caught in a steel trap" and a country girl in a "scarlet cloak" (lxi). Byron continues (lxiii):

> Now justices of peace must judge all pieces
>   Of mischief of all kinds, and keep the game
> And morals of the country from caprices
>   Of those who have not a license for the same;
> And of all things, excepting tithes and leases,
>   Perhaps these are most difficult to tame:
> Preserving partridges and pretty wenches
> Are puzzles to the most precautious benches.

These activities, together with the breeding of prize pigs and horses, were quite enough (lxviii–lxix) to keep Lord Henry occupied between his electioneering campaigns.

Byron uses Lord Henry as an example also of English politicians and statesmen. As an electioneer, Lord Henry was an indefatigable burrower for boroughs (XVI, lxx). His word of honor was inviolate (lxxi):

> Courteous and cautious therefore in his county,
>   He was all things to all men, and dispensed
> To some civility, to others bounty,
>   And promises to all—which last commenced
> To gather to a somewhat large amount, he
>   Not calculating how much they condensed;
> But what with keeping some, and breaking others,
> His word had the same value as another's.

Ambiguously enough, he was a friend both to "free-dom" and to "government" and, owing to his nice ability to discriminate, he was able to hit "exactly the just me-dium" between "place and patriotism" (lxxii). However, to please his sovereign, he was forced against his will to hold some sinecures "he wish'd abolish'd" (lxxii). Lord Henry heartily approved of innovation and progress, but he would not for a moment consider treading a "factious path to praise." With an admirable spirit of patient resig-nation he admitted (lxxiii) that the fatigue of his position was "greater than the profit." "Profit he cared not for, let others reap it" (lxxv). In short, Lord Henry was as independent as those who "were not paid for independ-ence," such as the common soldier or the common whore who has ascendance over the "irregulars in lust or gore" (lxxvi). And Byron concludes his satiric portrait with the comment (lxxvi):

> Thus on the mob all statesmen are as eager
> To prove their pride, as footmen to a beggar.

From satire of politicians Byron passes to satire of poli-tics. Byron, who was by virtue of his liberal inclinations a Whig, shared the prevailing Whig disgruntlement with the Tory government. In discussing the transience of things human in the "I have seen" stanzas, he remarks (XI, lxxxii):

> Nought's permanent among the human race,
> Except the Whigs *not* getting into place.

And he characterizes the party politics of Great Britain in a couplet (XII, xxiv):

> All countries have their "Lions," but in thee
> There is but one superb menagerie.

As an illustration of political chicanery Byron gives an extended description (XVI, lxxviii–ciii) of Lord and Lady

Amundeville's electioneering banquet. It is too long to quote here, but suffice it to say that it is a vigorous and faithful exposure of the sham and deceit and manipulation which, according to Byron's notion, attended the operation of party politics in his day.

The "Blues" Byron despised heartily. He had married one, and that intimate experience with their ilk had not increased his affection for these pseudo-literary ladies, the fashionable female intelligentsia of his day. His ridicule of Lady Byron's "blueness" I have already noted.

Byron's satire, "The Blues," is an example of his earlier satire on the "Blues," on Wordsworth and Southey, and on London "literary" society some years before he was doing the same thing in *Don Juan*. The particular "blue" lady of this earlier satire is suggestive of Miss Milbanke.

In Canto XI (1) Byron allows his hero to fall into the hands of the "Blues":

> The Blues, that tender tribe, who sigh o'er sonnets,
>   And with the pages of the last Review
> Line the interior of their heads or bonnets,
>   Advanced in all their azure's highest hue:
> They talk'd bad French or Spanish, and upon its
>   Late authors ask'd him for a hint or two;
> And which was softest, Russian or Castilian?
> And whether in his travels he saw Ilion?

But, fortunately, Juan emerges unscathed from his "deadly peril amongst live poets and blue ladies" (XI, lxiv).

Later, Byron contrasts Lady Adeline's actual literary talent with that of the "dilletanti" (XVI, xliv). She also had a "twilight tinge of 'Blue' " but was remote from that "sublimer azure hue" and was "weak enough to deem Pope a great poet" (XVI, xlvii).

Of Byron's satire of England and things English there remains for our consideration his satire of London.

Juan, newly arrived in England, stands on Shooter's Hill, overlooking London Town. What he sees is recorded (X, lxxxii) in Byron's rather unfeeling description of the great metropolis of his native country:

> A mighty mass of brick, and smoke, and shipping,
>   Dirty and dusky, but as wide as eye
> Could reach, with here and there a sail just skipping
>   In sight, then lost amidst the forestry
> Of masts; a wilderness of steeples peeping
>   On tiptoe through their sea-coal canopy;
> A huge, dun cupola, like a foolscap crown
> On a fool's head—and there is London Town.

Byron continues his disparagement of London in the opening stanzas of Canto XI. He describes it as that "vale of good and ill" where "London streets ferment in full activity" (XI, viii). It is the "mighty Babylon" of cities (XI, xxiii) and "that pleasant place where every kind of mischief's daily brewing" (XII, xxiii). The voice of the Thames can scarcely be heard through the clamor of English profanity (XI, xxiv).

Byron then (XI, xx–xxix) names all the famous sights of London, and though the dominant tone of the description is ridicule, there is a note of pride beneath his jeering.

Byron emphasizes the immorality of London by calling attention to the "pedestrian Paphians" who "abound in decent London" after dark and are "useful, like Malthus, in promoting marriage" (XI, xxx). He gives as his reason for making his references to London streets and squares anonymous that he cannot find a London square of the chastity of which he can be certain and of which "nothing naughty can be shown" (XIII, xxvi–xxvii).

As we have seen, Byron satirizes English government and national policy, English character, the much-boasted English freedom and morality, the artificiality of English "high society," English clergy, poets, lawyers, politicians, and statesmen, English politics, the "Blues," and London. Byron's apparent purpose in all this satire of England and things English is to expose the most despicable features of English society and character.

The two characteristics of the English society of Byron's day against which he inveighs most bitterly are cant—moral, religious, and political—and oppression. A passage from the Countess of Blessington's journal throws light on Byron's attitude:

> He on all occasions professes a detestation of what he calls *cant;* says it will banish from England all that is pure and good; and that while people are looking after the shadow, they lose the substance of goodness; he says that the best mode left for conquering it, is to expose it to *ridicule,* the only *weapon,* added he, that the English climate cannot rust.[38]

And two more brief quotations from the same source are illuminating. Referring to the English, Byron said to Lady Blessington: "Nothing amuses me more than to see refinement *versus* morals, and to know that people are shocked *not* at crimes, but their detection."[39] Elsewhere he says: "It is my respect for morals that makes me so indignant against its vile substitute cant, with which I wage war . . . ."[40]

Byron was the sworn enemy of bigotry and insincerity and oppression wherever he found them—in government, in foreign policy, in party politics, in the professions, or in society. And these abuses abounded in the England of his day. "The morals of English aristocratic society in the Eighteenth and early Nineteenth century . . . . were in essentials those of the Restoration, and hardly less fla-

[38] Blessington, *op. cit.,* p. 12.
[39] *Ibid.,* p. 328.   [40] *Ibid.,* p. 299.

grantly paraded."[41]   The criticism which Byron chiefly emphasizes in his satire of England is the imperfection of morality and freedom in the country which is supposed to be the freest and most moral.   In short, Byron's satire of England and things English has, in common with his satire of individuals, two major objectives: the ridicule of all insincerity and the denunciation of all that obstructs individual and national freedom.

IV

SATIRE OF INSTITUTIONS AND MODERN SOCIETY

The chief institutions which Byron satirizes in his *Don Juan* are war, despotism, and marriage. Let us examine his satire of these institutions in order to see if his purpose coincides with the two major objectives which we have noted in his satire of individuals and of England.

War, declares Byron (IV, cv), is the result of the "wild instinct of gore and glory" of "those blood-hounds," the militarists. And, in consequence, the earth has known "those sufferings Dante saw in hell alone."

Cantos VII and VIII of *Don Juan* contain Byron's most vigorous and extended satiric treatment of war. On the day on which Byron finished these two cantos, August 8, 1822, he wrote to Thomas Moore:

These contain a full detail (like the storm in Canto Second) of the siege and assault of Ismail, with much of sarcasm on those butchers in large business, your mercenary soldiery. . . . . With these things and these fellows, it is necessary, in the present clash of philosophy and tyranny, to throw away the scabbard.[42]

[41] Walter Alwyn Briscoe (Ed.), *Byron, the Poet. A Collection of Essays and Addresses* (London: G. Routledge and Sons, Ltd., 1924), p. 61.

[42] Prothero, *op. cit.*, VI, 101. (To Thomas Moore. Pisa, August 8, 1822.)

The first reference in Canto VII to the mercenary soldier is in his description (xviii) of the Russian army:

> Then there were foreigners of much renown,
> Of various nations, and all volunteers;
> Not fighting for their country or its crown,
> But wishing to be one day brigadiers;
> Also to have the sacking of a town;
> A pleasant thing to young men of their years.

A few stanzas farther on in the same canto he ridicules (lxiv) the mercenary soldier as one whose "high, heroic bosom burn'd for cash and conquest." And again he inveighs against the mercenary soldiery who slay millions "for their ration" (VIII, lxviii). Their lust for slaughter and love of plunder draw Byron's scathing denunciation (VIII, cii–ciii and cxxiv–cxxix).

All through the description of the siege of Ismail Byron emphasizes the callousness and heartlessness of war. A soldier's reward for the sacrifice of his life on the battlefield is "three lines" in a bulletin (VII, xx). Apropos of this, Byron wonders if "a man's name in a *bulletin* may make up for a *bullet in* his body?" (VII, xxi). Byron condemns (VII, xxxi) the callousness which is displayed in the perfunctory listing in the gazettes of the names of the war dead. There is also the unknown soldier whose name receives not even the meager honor of mention in a "gazette of slaughter" (VII, xxxi and xxxiv; also VIII, xviii).

The indiscriminate ruthlessness of war, which inflicts suffering upon innocent noncombatants as well as participants, evokes Byron's sarcasm (VII, xxiii):

> The Russians, having built two batteries on
> An isle near Ismail, had two ends in view;
> The first was to bombard it, and knock down
> The public buildings and the private too,

> No matter what poor souls might be undone.
> The city's shape suggested this, 'tis true;
> Form'd like an amphitheatre, each dwelling
> Presented a fine mark to throw a shell in.

Byron epitomizes in a single line (VII, xli) the thoroughgoing destruction wrought by war:

> For war cuts up not only branch, but root.

Like some of the poets of the First World War, Byron portrays (VIII, xii–xiii) the sheer, brutal horror of war:

> Three hundred cannon threw up their emetic,
>   And thirty thousand muskets flung their pills
> Like hail, to make a bloody diuretic.
>   Mortality! thou hast thy monthly bills:
> Thy plagues, thy famines, thy physicians, yet tick,
>   Like the death-watch, within our ears the ills
> Past, present, and to come;—but all may yield
> To the true portrait of one battle-field;
>
> There the still varying pangs, which multiply
>   Until their very number makes men hard
> By the infinities of agony,
>   Which meet the gaze, whate'er it may regard—
> The groan, the roll in dust, the all-white eye
>   Turn'd back within its socket,—these reward
> Your rank and file by thousands, while the rest
> May win perhaps a riband at the breast!

The ugly picture continues (xix–xx), complete in every bloody detail:

> Juan and Johnson join'd a certain corps,
>   And fought away with might and main, not knowing
> The way which they had never tried before,
>   And still less guessing where they might be going;
> But on they march'd, dead bodies trampling o'er,
>   Firing, and thrusting, slashing, sweating, glowing,
> But fighting thoughtlessly enough to win,
> To their *two* selves, *one* whole bright bulletin.

> Thus on they wallow'd in the bloody mire
>   Of dead and dying thousands,—sometimes gaining
> A yard or two of ground, which brought them nigher
>   To some odd angle for which all were straining;
> At other times, repulsed by the close fire,
>   Which really poured as if all hell were raining
> Instead of heaven, they stumbled backwards o'er
> A wounded comrade, sprawling in his gore.

The crimes of depredation and rapine and plunder which follow the taking of a besieged city do not escape Byron (VIII, lxxxiii and lxxxviii):

> The city's taken—only part by part—
>   And death is drunk with gore: there's not a street
> Where fights not to the last some desperate heart
>   For those for whom it soon shall cease to beat.
> Here War forgot his own destructive art
>   In more destroying Nature; and the heat
> Of carnage, like the Nile's sun-sodden slime,
> Engender'd monstrous shapes of every crime.
>
> . . . .
> . . . .
>
> The bayonet pierces and the sabre cleaves,
>   And human lives are lavish'd everywhere,
> As the year closing whirls the scarlet leaves
>   When the stripp'd forest bows to the bleak air,
> And groans; and thus the peopled city grieves,
>   Shorn of its best and loveliest, and left bare;
> But still it falls in vast and awful splinters,
> As oaks blown down with all their thousand winters.

And Byron concludes this picture of war's horror and desolation with this stanza (cxxiii) in which he hints at all the dark horrors and unnatural crimes which ensue when an assaulted city is taken:

> All that the mind would shrink from of excesses;
>   All that the body perpetrates of bad;

All that we read, hear, dream, of man's distresses;
   All that the devil would do if run stark mad;
All that defies the worst which pen expresses;
   All by which hell is peopled, or as sad
As hell—mere mortals who their power abuse—
Was here (as heretofore and since) let loose.

Byron satirizes military leaders and officers also. He takes Suwarrow as a typical example and gives us in one stanza (VII, lviii) a vivid sketch of Suwarrow and an ironic epitome of the "noble art of killing." Great military leaders, he says (VII, lxviii), "for one sole leaf" of the imaginary laurel tree of fame have not hesitated to set flowing an "unebbing sea" of "blood and tears." Such a one was Suwarrow (lxxvii):

   —who but saw things in the gross,
Being much too gross to see them in detail,
Who calculated life as so much dross,
   And as the wind a widow'd nation's wail—

Byron denounces not only the military leaders but also the idle and wealthy noncombatants who sit at home dining and drinking while the youth of the land give up their lives on the battlefield. During the last war, he says (XIII, liii, liv),

the News abounded
More with these dinners than the kill'd or wounded;—

As thus: "On Thursday there was a grand dinner;
   Present, Lords A. B. C."—Earls, dukes, by name
Announced with no less pomp than victory's winner:
   Then underneath, and in the very same
Column: date, "Falmouth. There has lately been here
   The Slap-dash regiment, so well known to fame,
Whose loss in the late action we regret:
The vacancies are fill'd up—see Gazette."

This stanza is comparable with the withering irony of a poem of the First World War, "Base Details," by Siegfried Sassoon.

Again Byron's satire of the institution of war has a truly modern ring when he brands (XII, v–vi) the great financiers as the actual war lords of Europe:

> Who hold the balance of the world? Who reign
>   O'er congress, whether royalist or liberal?
> Who rouse the shirtless patriots of Spain?
>   (That make old Europe's journals squeak and
>   gibber all).
> Who keep the world, both old and new, in pain
>   Or pleasure? Who make politics run glibber all?
> The shade of Buonaparte's noble daring?—
> Jew Rothschild, and his fellow-Christian, Baring.
>
> Those, and the truly liberal Lafitte,
>   Are the true lords of Europe. Every loan
> Is not a merely speculative hit,
>   But seats a nation or upsets a throne.

In the closing stanzas of Canto VII Byron provides a vigorous unmasking of war. He facetiously suggests that there may have been some romance in Homeric warfare but that any romantic element has long since vanished. At any rate, if the Ancients had more glory in their warfare, "still we moderns equal you in blood" (lxxx). There is fine irony in his invoking (lxxxii) of the shades of illustrious warriors of the past:

> Oh, ye great bulletins of Bonaparte!
>   Oh, ye less grand long lists of kill'd and wounded!
> Shade of Leonidas, who fought so hearty,
>   When my poor Greece was once, as now, surrounded!
> Oh, Caesar's Commentaries! now impart, ye
>   Shadows of glory! (lest I be confounded),
> A portion of your fading twilight hues,
> So beautiful, so fleeting, to the Muse.

Byron strips the tinsel and the sentiment from war and reveals its naked deformity (lxxxiv):

> Medals, rank, ribands, lace, embroidery, scarlet,
> Are things immortal to immortal man,
> As purple to the Babylonian harlot:
> An uniform to boys is like a fan
> To women; there is scarce a crimson varlet
> But deems himself the first in Glory's van.
> But Glory's glory; and if you would find
> What that is—ask the pig who sees the wind!

He continues his exposure of the true nature of that ambiguous institution, sometimes called "murder" and at other times "glory" (VII, xxvi), in the opening stanza of Canto VIII:

> Oh, blood and thunder! and oh, blood and wounds!
> These are but vulgar oaths, as you may deem,
> Too gentle reader! and most shocking sounds:
> And so they are; yet thus is Glory's dream
> Unriddled, and as my true Muse expounds
> At present such things, since they are her theme,
> So be they her inspirers! Call them Mars,
> Bellona, what you will—they mean but wars.

On the battlefield, Byron observes, "courage does not glow so much as under a triumphal arch" (VIII, xxi). War, he declares (xlii), is "hell" in spite of what people say

> Of glory, and all that immortal stuff
> Which daily fills a regiment (besides their pay,
> That daily shilling which makes warriors tough)—

Byron emphasizes (I, cxxxii) the senselessness of war and its total lack of constructive benefit for mankind:

> This is the patent age of new inventions
> For killing bodies, and for saving souls,
> All propagated with the best intentions;
> Sir Humphry Davy's lantern, by which coals

> Are safely mined for in the mode he mentions,
> Timbuctoo travels, voyages to the Poles,
> Are ways to benefit mankind, as true,
> Perhaps, as shooting them at Waterloo.

He continues this emphasis in the following stanza in which he points to the tremendous price paid and the insignificant gain—the drying up of a single tear is of more importance than the shedding of seas of gore (VIII, iii):

> History can only take things in the gross;
> But could we know them in detail, perchance
> In balancing the profit and the loss,
> War's merit it by no means might enhance,
> To waste so much gold for a little dross,
> As hath been done, mere conquest to advance.
> The drying up a single tear has more
> Of honest fame, than shedding seas of gore.

"*One* life saved," Byron avows (IX, xxxiv),

> is a thing to recollect
> Far sweeter than the greenest laurels sprung
> From the manure of human clay, though deck'd
> With all the praises ever said or sung:

Nor does Byron neglect to ridicule the blind mob spirit and hysteria which accompany war. He impugns (VIII, xxxviii) that

> odd impulse, which in wars or creeds
> Makes men, like cattle, follow him who leads.

And, finally, Byron shows himself not entirely a pacifist, for he justifies one kind of war, "defence of freedom, country, or of laws." All other war he denounces (VII, xl) as "mere lust of power." Wars, he says, "except in freedom's battles," are nothing but "a child of Murder's rattles" (VIII, iv), and continues (v):

And such they are—and such they will be found:
  Not so Leonidas and Washington,
Whose every battle-field is holy ground,
  Which breathes of nations saved, not worlds undone.
How sweetly on the ear such echoes sound!
  While the mere victor's may appal or stun
The servile and the vain, such names will be
A watchword till the future shall be free.

It has been demonstrated, then, that Byron in *Don Juan* satirizes the institution of war most vigorously. He condemns its mercenary aspect, its callousness and heartlessness, its indiscriminate ruthlessness, its sheer horror and sordidness, its meaningless brutality, its ambiguous and anomalous glory, its entire lack of constructive value, its enormous cost, its senselessness and futility, the ignorance from which it springs, and the hysteria by which it is nurtured. Only wars of liberation and wars waged in defense of country are justifiable.

This is Byron's mature attitude toward war.[43] He proves himself to be one of the greatest of satirists of war in English poetry. He is comparable with Shelley in this respect, and with Wordsworth in that poet's early writing. The attitude of these poets is far in advance of their age. It is like that of the leading British poets of the First World War—Graves, Gibson, Sassoon, Owen, and others, who portray war in all its barbarity, senselessness, and futility.

Passing on now to Byron's satire of despotism, it is to be observed that he frequently contrasts *despotism* with *true kingship*. Byron minces no words in pronouncing judgment upon all despots. They are worse than barbarians, for they are not only the enemies of physical

---

[43] In his poem, "The Devil's Drive" (1814), Byron first gave satiric expression to what later became a frequent theme—the horror of war.

progress but the deadliest foes of Thought. He swears
(IX, xxiii–xxiv) his plain, downright detestation of all
despotism:

> For me, I deem an absolute autocrat
> *Not* a barbarian, but much worse than that.

> And I will war, at least in words (and—should
>   My chance so happen—deeds), with all who war
> With Thought;—and of Thought's foes by far most rude,
>   Tyrants and sycophants have been and are.
> I know not who may conquer: if I could
>   Have such a prescience, it should be no bar
> To this my plain, sworn, downright detestation
> Of every despotism in every nation.

This is Byron's war cry against all oppression. And
how consistent and unrelenting was his warfare, both in
words and deeds, against all that hampers individual and
national freedom, we well know!

Despotism abounded in Byron's day. "Kings despotic,"
he asserts (IV, vi), have not become "obsolete" as have
"true knights," "chaste dames," and other "fancies" of the
age of chivalry. He holds despots responsible for the
savagery of modern warfare; it is they who "employ all
arts to teach their subjects to destroy" (VIII, xcii). Thou-
sands slain scarce quench the insatiable thirst of tyrants for
conquest. "Blood only serves to wash Ambition's hands!"
(IX, lix). The human heart shudders at the horrors which
"things call'd sovereigns" perpetrate (IX, lx). If modern
despots differ in any respect from their predecessors it is
in that they "*now* at least must *talk* of law before they
butcher" (X, lxxiv).

But Byron foresees (XVI, x) a time when despotism
will be obliterated from human society:

> So perish every tyrant's robe piece-meal!

Byron hints (VI, xiii) the ultimate fate of all despots in his remarks about the Turkish Sultan:

> His Highness, the sublimest of mankind,—
> So styled according to the usual forms
> Of every monarch, till they are consigned
> To those sad hungry Jacobins the worms,
> Who on the very loftiest kings have dined,—

Death, "the sovereign's sovereign," and the great "reformer," eventually levels even despots to the estate of their oppressed subjects (X, xxv):

> And death, the sovereign's sovereign, though the great
> Gracchus of all mortality, who levels,
> With his *Agrarian* laws, the high estate
> Of him who feasts, and fights, and roars, and revels,
> To one small grass-grown patch (which must await
> Corruption for its crop), with the poor devils
> Who never had a foot of land till now,—
> Death's a reformer, all men must allow.

But Byron is not content to await the coming of the great "reformer"; he urges (VIII, cxxxv) the people to rise against "earth's tyrants."

> For I will teach, if possible, the stones
> To rise against earth's tyrants. Never let it
> Be said that we still truckle unto thrones;—

And he is confident (VIII, cxxxvii) that thrones and despots will become "the pleasant riddles of futurity" when men shall regard them as the "mammoth's bones" or "hieroglyphics on Egyptian stones," wondering "what old world such things could see." Another evidence that Byron looked upon despotism as a doomed institution is found in his expression, "the *setting* sun of tyranny" (XV, xxii).

Byron refuses to have any part in the perpetuation of the institution of despotism. He will not lend his voice to "slavery's jackal cry" or become one of the "human insects" who are "catering for spiders"—the tyrants (IX, xxvi–xxvii). On the contrary, he very definitely reveals his interest in political reformation. It makes (XV, xcii) his

> blood boil like the springs of Hecla,
> To see men let these scoundrel sovereigns break law.

And, finally, Byron contrasts (XII, lxxxiii) despotism with the only *true* kingship, constitutional possession of a throne; but even that is but a step toward the achievement of complete freedom:

> He saw, however, at the closing session,
>   That noble sight, when *really* free the nation,
> A king in constitutional possession
>   Of such a throne as is the proudest station,
> Though despots know it not—till the progression
>   Of freedom shall complete their education.
> 'Tis not mere splendour makes the show august
> To eye or heart—it is the people's trust.

It is easy to see that Byron's satire of despotism is motivated by his thoroughgoing and unqualified hatred of all that interferes with individual and national independence.[44]

Marriage is the third target of Byron's satire of institutions. But his satire of marriage differs in two important respects from his satire of war and despotism. In the case of marriage it is the abuses in the institution which he attacks and not the institution itself. Furthermore, marriage is the one of the three institutions which had most injured Byron. Hence his satire of it reflects the bias of his personal experience.

Byron recognizes that one of the common causes of marital infelicity is the marriage of youth with age; he has

[44] See also Byron's "Age of Bronze," which contains vigorous denunciation of "Legitimacy."

Juan fall in love (I, cvii) with the young and beautiful
Julia, who is married to a man more than twice her years.
It is the perfunctory and mercenary nature of much of the
marriage in Byron's own class of society against which he
inveighs (I, lxv).

> Alfonso was the name of Julia's lord,
>   A man well looking for his year's, and who
> Was neither much beloved nor yet abhorr'd:
>   They lived together as most people do,
> Suffering each other's foibles by accord,
>   And not exactly either *one* or *two;*

Byron also ridicules (I, lxiv) the tendency in "the
moral North" to parade matrimonial difficulties in the
courtroom:

> Happy the nations of the moral North!
>   Where all is virtue, and the winter season
> Sends sin, without a rag on, shivering forth
>   ('Twas snow that brought St. Anthony to reason);
> Where juries cast up what a wife is worth,
>   By laying whate'er sum, in mulct, they please on
> The lover, who must pay a handsome price,
> Because it is a marketable vice.

Most marriage, Byron avers (XI, lxxxix), is of the
"lawful, awful wedlock" variety which has as its prosaic
obligation the regular "peopling" of the earth. It is this
kind of marriage—this "marketable vice"—of which he
paints an extended picture in his description of the "marriage market" in Canto XII, stanzas xxxi–xxxvii. Young
women are virtually sold to the highest bidder by their
ambitious and mercenary mothers.

The fate of the young unmarried man is much the same,
for he has an awkward time of it (XII, lviii) in trying to
please the ladies who have such "separate" aims, the single
ladies "wishing to be double" and the married ones "to

save the virgins trouble." The young man's fate is often
thus (lx):

> Perhaps you'll have a letter from the mother,
>   To say her daughter's feelings are trepann'd;
> Perhaps you'll have a visit from the brother,
>   All strut, and stays, and whiskers, to demand
> What "your intentions are?"—One way or other
>   It seems the virgin's heart expects your hand:
> And between pity for her case and yours,
> You'll add to Matrimony's list of cures.

Byron is obviously sincere when he deplores (III, v)
the fact that marriage and love are so frequently antitheti-
cal:

> 'Tis melancholy, and a fearful sign
> Of human frailty, folly, also crime,
> That love and marriage rarely can combine,
>   Although they both are born in the same clime;
> Marriage from love, like vinegar from wine—
>   A sad, sour, sober beverage—by time
> Is sharpen'd from its high celestial flavour,
> Down to a very homely household savour.

And he points out (XV, xli) the reason for this antithe-
sis; marriage, as he had encountered it in society and in
his own personal experience, was too frequently regarded
as the end of romance and the beginning of a prosaic, de-
vitalized, passionless relationship, shorn of all joyousness
and zest:

> Love's riotous, but marriage should have quiet,
> And being consumptive, live on a milk diet.

"For instance," he says, "passion in a lover's glorious,"
but "in a husband is pronounced uxorious" (III, vi).

Byron's own unfortunate marital experience colors all
his view of marriage. Marriage is without romance;
there's something in "domestic doings" which is incompatible with "wooings" and no one "cares for matrimonial

cooings" (III, viii). All "comedies," he observes, are
"ended by a marriage" (III, ix). The poets do not write of
marriage but of courtship (III, ix); as for exceptions (x):

> The only two that in my recollection
>   Have sung of heaven and hell, or marriage, are
> Dante and Milton, and of both the affection
>   Was hapless in their nuptials, for some bar
> Of fault or temper ruin'd the connexion
>   (Such things, in fact, it don't ask much to mar);
> But Dante's Beatrice and Milton's Eve
> Were not drawn from their spouses, you conceive.

There are frequent veiled allusions to his own unhappy
marital experience in his satire of marriage. In the description of Lambro's return (III, li) is one of the more obvious allusions to his own experience. His disillusionment
is even more evident in his ironical comparison of Eastern
polygamy with Western monogamy; he suggests (V,
clviii) that the East might learn a lesson from the West:

> Why don't they knead two virtuous souls for life
> Into that moral centaur, man and wife?

Another gibe of this nature is his remark (VI, lxxiii)
that Juan, in his female disguise in the harem, lay as fast
asleep beside Dudu as ever "husband by his mate in holy
matrimony snores away." And several others in this ironic
vein are as follows: marriage like war is inevitably followed by "discord" (VII, xlix); Haidée was "as pure as
Psyche ere she grew a wife—" (III, lxxiv); "Chaste
dames" are among the "fancies" of an earlier time which
now are "obsolete" (IV, vi); and among the various kinds
of love is a third sort (IX, lxxvi) which flourishes in
"every Christian land," namely,

> when chaste matrons to their other ties,
> Add what may be call'd *marriage in disguise.*

There are many others, too numerous to mention.

Byron indulges in a bantering commentary (XV, xxxv–
xxxvi) on Rapp, the Harmonist, and his views of marriage.
Why, asks Byron, did Rapp call a "state sans wedlock
. . . . Harmony?" Apparently, he regarded marriage and
harmony as incompatible.

Another characteristic of marriage in Byron's conception of the institution was servitude or bondage. Speaking
of the wedding ring, he denounces it (IX, lxx) as the
symbol of bondage and "the damn'dest part of matrimony." And again (III, vii):

> The same things cannot always be admired,
> Yet 'tis "so nominated in the bond,"
> That both are tied till one shall have expired.

Thus Byron's attack on marriage is directed against its
mercenary aspect, its perfunctoriness, its want of romance
and love and consequent infidelity, and its bondage. But
that he was able to conceive of the true marital happiness
of two sincerely devoted persons can be readily substan-
tiated by his attitude toward Teresa Guiccioli as well as
by his own emphasis of the distinction between true marriage and loveless wedlock in his poetry and in his conversations. He said to Lady Blessington:

> Were the Contessa Guiccioli and I married, we should, I am
> sure, be cited as an example of conjugal happiness, and the domes-
> tic and retired life we lead would entitle us to respect; but our
> union, wanting the legal and religious part of the ceremony of
> marriage, draws on us both censure and blame. She is formed to
> make a good wife to any man to whom she attached herself. She
> is fond of retirement—is of a most affectionate disposition—and
> noble-minded and disinterested to the highest degree . . . . When
> passion is replaced by better feelings—those of affection, friend-
> ship, and confidence—when, in short, the *liaison* has all of mar-
> riage but its forms, then it is that we wish to give it the respecta-
> bility of wedlock.[45]

[45] Blessington, *op. cit.*, pp. 115–16.

And at another time Byron, speaking of marriage, said to her:

If people like each other so well as not to be able to live asunder, this is the only tie that can assure happiness—all others entail misery.[46]

Byron states definitely his position with regard to marriage in a stanza (XII, xv) from *Don Juan* in which he grants that love and marriage may exist together, "and *should* ever"; but, unfortunately, marriage may also exist without love—and all too frequently does:

> Is not all love prohibited whatever,
> Excepting marriage? which is love, no doubt,
> After a sort; but somehow people never
> With the same thought the two words have help'd out.
> Love may exist *with* marriage, and *should* ever,
> And marriage also may exist without;

Byron reveals his esteem for true marriage in contradistinction to the intrigues and petty passions "of the common school" (IV, xvii) when he refers (XIV, xcv) to "the marriage state" as "the best or worst of any." It was because he did have a sincere regard for real love that he was so keenly alert to the notorious abuses in the institution of marriage and attacked them so relentlessly.

We may say, then, that Byron's satire of marriage is motivated by the same strong feelings which evoked his satire of other institutions—his love of liberty and his detestation of insincerity. He denounces war because it is not only barbarous but irrational and futile. He despises despotism because it is incompatible with individual and national liberty. And he pours out sarcasm upon marriage because to him it spells hypocrisy and bondage.

Closely associated with Byron's satire of institutions, in fact an extension of the same, is his satire of modern

---

[46] *Ibid.,* pp. 141–42.

society in general. He satirizes his own epoch with its con-
fusion, uncertainty, and unrest.[47] It is an age, he declares
(XIV, lxxxiv), which is mad:

> Shut up the world at large, let Bedlam out;
> And you will be perhaps surprised to find
> All things pursue exactly the same route,
> As now with those of *soi-disant* sound mind.

It is an age of iron-handed despotism and seething unrest. Byron takes us across Europe, in his description of
Juan's journey from Russia to England (X, lviii ff.),
pointing out the oppression and misery which exist in the
various European countries. Poland and Warsaw he mentions as famous for "yokes of iron" (X, lviii). Germany
he refers to (X, lx) as the country

> whose somewhat tardy millions
> Have princes who spur more than their postilions.

Holland, "that water-land of Dutchmen and of ditches,"
is a country where the common people have only a "cor-
dial," since the "good government" has deprived them
of all else (X, lxiii).

He denounces the servile attitude of the Irish toward
the English king (XI, xxxviii),[48] and praises Greece and
Spain as the only two nations "strongly stinging to be free"
from despotism and oppression (IX, xxviii). He stigma-
tizes the Congress of Verona with this line: "I have seen
a Congress doing all that's mean" (XI, lxxxiv).[49]

This modern age, Byron reiterates, is not a heroic one.
It possesses no sublimity. For this reason a poet is hard
put to sing its praises. A poet is obliged to color with nature
"manners that are artificial." Gone are the days when

[47] Byron's most concentrated satirical attack on his age is in his "Age
of Bronze." See *Poetical Works,* pp. 165–73.

[48] Cf. Byron's "The Irish Avatar," stanza xiv.

[49] See Byron's "The Age of Bronze," in *Poetical Works,* p. 169.

"men made the manners"; quite the opposite is now true
(XV, xxv–xxvi):

> But "laissez aller"—knights and dames I sing,
> 　Such as the times may furnish. 'Tis a flight
> Which seems at first to need no lofty wing,
> 　Plumed by Longinus or the Stagyrite:
> The difficulty lies in colouring
> 　(Keeping the due proportions still in sight)
> With nature manners which are artificial,
> And rend'ring general that which is especial.
>
> The difference is, that in the days of old
> 　Men made the manners; manners now make men—
> Pinn'd like a flock, and fleeced too in their fold,
> 　At least nine, and a ninth beside of ten.
> Now this at all events must render cold
> 　Your writers, who must either draw again
> Days better drawn before, or else assume
> The present, with their common-place costume.

It is an age, he insists (VI, lvi), of "Corinthian Brass,"
which was, he adds, "a mixture of all metals, but the
brazen uppermost."[50]

There is a Rousseauistic flavor to Byron's condemnation
of modern society. He denounces society (IV, xxviii) as

> these thick solitudes
> Call'd social, haunts of Hate, and Vice, and Care;

Society, he avows (V, xxv), destroys whatever altru-
istic feeling is latent in men's hearts:

> Society itself, which should create
> 　Kindness, destroys what little we had got:
> To feel for none is the true social art
> Of the world's stoics—men without a heart.

He gives fuller expression to this theme in Canto VIII

[50] *Ibid.*

(lxi–lxii) where he contrasts the natural, simple, and noble life of Daniel Boone, and other American frontiersmen, with the "savage" life of modern men:

> Of all men, saving Sylla the man-slayer,
>   Who passes for in life and death most lucky,
> Of the great names which in our faces stare,
>   The General Boon, back-woodsman of Kentucky,
> Was happiest amongst mortals anywhere;
>   For killing nothing but a bear or buck, he
> Enjoy'd the lonely, vigorous, harmless days
> Of his old age in wilds of deepest maze.
>
> Crime came not near him—she is not the child
>   Of solitude; Health shrank not from him—for
> Her home is in the rarely trodden wild,
>   Where if men seek her not, and death be more
> Their choice than life, forgive them, as beguiled
>   By habit to what their own hearts abhor—
> In cities caged. The present case in point I
> Cite is, that Boon lived hunting up to ninety;

He extols (VIII, lxv–lxvi) the natural life of these people with its freedom from the accompaniments of modern civilization—war, disease, and greed:

> He was not all alone: around him grew
>   A sylvan tribe of children of the chase,
> Whose young, unawaken'd world was ever new,
>   Nor sword nor sorrow yet had left a trace
> On her unwrinkled brow, nor could you view
>   A frown on Nature's or on human face;
> The free-born forest found and kept them free,
> And fresh as is a torrent or a tree.
>
> And tall, and strong, and swift of foot were they,
>   Beyond the dwarfing city's pale abortions,
> Because their thoughts had never been the prey
>   Of care or gain: the green woods were their portions;

No sinking spirits told them they grew grey,
  No fashion made them apes of her distortions;
Simple they were, not savage; and their rifles,
  Though very true, were not yet used for trifles.

And he satirizes (lxvii) the corruption, ambition, and artificiality of modern life in his praise of natural life:

Motion was in their days, rest in their slumbers
  And cheerfulness the handmaid of their toil;
Nor yet too many nor too few their numbers;
  Corruption could not make their hearts her soil;
The lust which stings, the splendour which encumbers,
  With the free foresters divide no spoil;
Serene, not sullen, were the solitudes
Of this unsighing people of the woods.

Byron concludes his sweeping satire of modern society, with all its "sweet" consequences of war, disease, ambition, lust, oppression, and discontent, in these words (VIII, lxviii):

So much for Nature:—by way of variety,
  Now back to thy great joys, Civilisation!
And the sweet consequence of large society,
  War, pestilence, the despot's desolation,
The kingly scourge, the lust of notoriety,
  The millions slain by soldiers for their ration,
The scenes like Catherine's boudoir at three-score,
With Ismail's storm to soften it the more.

To recapitulate briefly the objects of Byron's satire in *Don Juan* before proceeding to an estimate of its significance, Byron's satire, whether of individuals, nations, institutions, or modern society in general, is consistently directed against all insincerity and all which obstructs individual and national freedom. It is reasonable to conclude, then, that Byron's satiric performance in *Don Juan* tallies with his statement of his satiric purpose, *"Don Juan* will be known by and bye, for what it is intended,—a *Satire* on *abuses* of the present states of Society . . . ."[51]

IV

THE IMPORT OF *DON JUAN*

A second major consideration of this study is an evaluation of the significance of Byron's satire in *Don Juan*. The evidence already accumulated tends to correct the misconception that Byron's attitude toward the great problems of existence is wholly negative. Certainly Byron's vigorous and unequivocal denunciation of hypocrisy and insincerity in individuals, of essential unsoundness or flagrant abuses in social institutions, and of the worst features of modern civilization cannot be regarded as other than constructive in implication and effect. If Byron's mature satire is occasionally cynical, it concerns shameless human nature and human institutions. The gross and inhuman oppression of tyranny, the insatiable avarice, irrationality, and savagery of war, the pestilence, poverty, and polar inequalities of modern society—all these were evils so prevalent and so flagrant as readily to provoke cynicism. But certainly it is not reasonable to brand as "cynical" the satire which exposes and vigorously decries the evils of society. Byron's half-jocular claim to be regarded as a moral teacher is not to be dismissed at its face value. Byron fearlessly and uncompromisingly attacked the social evils of his day. The primary objects of his satire were insincerity and oppression. Stated positively, the major implications of his satire are sincerity and freedom. Assuredly the import of such satire is constructive.

The charge of cynicism is owing, at least in part, to Byron's habitual juxtaposition of the petty and the heroic,

[51] Prothero, *op. cit.*, VI, 155–56. (To John Murray. Genoa, December 25, 1822.)

the base and the virtuous. As I have indicated in my study of the contemporary periodical criticism of *Don Juan,* Byron's sudden plunges from the sublime to the ridiculous and his astonishing juxtapositions of virtue and vice were deplored as evidence of a cynical want of faith in the reality of virtue. The same criticism has been expressed by a modern critic, Hugh Walker. It is true, he says, that no man is a hero to his valet, because the valet sees his pettiness. But so much the worse for the valet. And, Walker continues, "so much the worse for the satirist if he imagines that the admixture of pettiness makes the heroism unreal."[52]

But this criticism is not applicable to Byron. For Byron the admixture of the vicious does *not* make virtue unreal. Byron's representation of the startling proximity in human nature of virtues and vices clearly was intended not to disprove the reality of virtue but rather to emphasize Byron's profound conviction of the insensible but inevitable decline of virtue through overconfidence in its strength. Byron attacks not virtue but false virtue. The often reiterated accusation of the contemporary reviews that Byron's purpose in *Don Juan* was to bring contempt upon, to undermine by ridicule, all that ennobles or delights mankind it is impossible to support except by the violent wresting of certain passages from their context. Byron attacks not ideals but false idealism, false sentiment, false loyalty, false morality, false patriotism, and false freedom. With keen insight and utter fearlessness he analyzes and exposes the contrasts and contradictions in human life and relentlessly tears down insincerity, pretense, and sham. Well might he exclaim, "Oh, for a *forty-parson power* to chant thy praise, Hypocrisy!" (X, xxxiv).

The charge of misanthropy is owing, largely, to Byron's forthrightness and plain speaking. He did not mince

[52] Walker, *op. cit.,* p. 271.

words. To him war meant plunder of the burdened tax-payers at home no less than of the enemy. To him war was at best a "brain-spattering, windpipe-slitting art" (IX, iv), engaged in by "those butchers in large business, your mercenary soldiery,"[53] at the beck and call of avaricious despots, burning with the lust of economic conquest. He saw, too, and did not hesitate to denounce, the great financiers as the true war lords of Europe. He stripped war of its honor and its glory and revealed its stark hideousness. His political views as well were heretical. He had no "proper" respect for tyrants and despots, and refused to acknowledge them as the wise, benign, and well-meaning guardians of the public weal. Furthermore, Byron was a zealot in his devotion to liberty, both individual and po-litical. His revolutionary indoctrination was regarded by his contemporaries as incendiary, seditious, and subversive. His works, they asserted, were full of treasonable state-ments such as

> For I will teach, if possible,
> The stones to rise against earth's tyrants!

And he even presumed to suggest that "the future shall be free!" He refused to preserve a discreet silence with regard to the vagaries and imperfections of "holy matri-mony." He also violated another time-honored belief—that women have so much the best of the bargain in life. He made bold to say that "man to man so oft unjust is always so to woman." And as for his ideas of ambition and success, they were as "degenerate" as his opinions of fame and glory were "perverse." He was utterly devoid of the attitude of veneration for worldly success. And most in-comprehensible of all to his contemporaries was his vehe-ment insistence that the age in which he lived was *not* the

---

[53] Prothero, *op. cit.*, VI, 101. (To Thomas Moore. Pisa, August 8, 1822.)

most urbane, cultured, enlightened, and democratic the world had seen![54]

These, then, are the characteristics of Byron's satire—thoroughgoing detestation of all that smacks of hypocrisy and forthright denunciation of the most notorious abuses in modern social institutions—which have been branded nihilism and misanthropy.

In speaking of the significance of Byron's satire in *Don Juan*, it is impossible to ignore the charge most frequently preferred against the poem—that it is immoral in tendency. The opinion of Karl Elze, with regard to this, represents a not uncommon view. He asserts that "sensual pleasure" is "the only thing which escapes the lash of his [Byron's] ridicule . . . ."[55] Hugh Walker's view coincides, in this respect, with Elze's. "Vice," he says, "is not explained away or excused by pronouncing the word satire. . . . . There is much in *Don Juan* which it would be sublime simplicity to believe to be there for the purpose of reformation."[56] Byron does seem to revel in the sensual pleasures which he so glamorously describes. But the undeniable sensuality of certain portions of the poem is definitely subordinate to the positive satiric significance of the poem as a whole. It is impossible to adduce evidence in support of the charge that the poem attempts to justify debauchery and defend vice. Byron attacks not virtue, but false virtue. Byron himself denied any conscious attempt to degrade morals. To the Countess of Blessington he said:

[54] Several of the ideas in this paragraph appear in an anonymous article on *Don Juan* in *Articles and Criticisms on Byron*, IV, 752–54. This is a collection of articles on Byron clipped from various early nineteenth-century periodicals and bound together in a unique set of volumes of which the Duke University Library has volumes 1, 2, and 4–8.

[55] Karl Elze, *Lord Byron* (London, 1872), p. 421.

[56] Walker, *op. cit.*, p. 276.

I was willing to plead guilty of having sometimes represented Vice under alluring forms; but it was so generally in the world, therefore it was necessary to paint it so; but that I never represented virtue under the sombre and disgusting shapes of dullness, severity, and *ennui*, and that I always took care to represent the votaries of vice as unhappy themselves, and entailing unhappiness on those that loved them; so that *my moral* was unexceptionable.[57]

This statement is borne out by *Don Juan*. What encouragement of vice can be discovered in Julia's lifelong misery and Haidée's horrible death? If the man comes off scatheless, that is the *world's* morality, and not Byron's. Juan, his hero, is not a selfish debaucher but an impressible, generous, affectionate youth, "more sinned against than sinning," who shows himself an admirer of innocence as much as of beauty. This is shown by his rescue of the little Turkish girl, his devotion to her, and his zeal for her welfare (VIII, xci–cii). It is also shown by his preference for the sweet, gentle, and virtuous Aurora Raby, who shone like a "star" among the feminine celebrities at Lady Adeline's house party (XV, xliii–lviii). Furthermore, Byron represents Haidée as an example of simple, naïve, natural love (II, ccii ff.), and Don Juan is true to her memory when assailed by the Sultan's favorite (V, cxvii). Likewise, Byron's statement is borne out by his consistent ridicule of conventional love, on the one hand, and his idyllic pictures of true love, on the other. When Byron writes seriously of woman he is at his best. As one critic has rightly said, "Indeed, the mere mention of true love between man and woman is generally enough to harmonise his verse and raise it toward sublimity."[58]

---

[57] Blessington, *op. cit.*, p. 33. This is very much like Fielding's defense in his preface to *Joseph Andrews;* see Everyman edition, pp. xlii–xliii.

[58] Sir G. Douglas, "*Don Juan* in Literature and Music," *Cornhill Magazine*, n.s. LI (July 1921), p. 102.

One may say, then, that in implication and essential effect Byron's social satire in *Don Juan* is constructive. Byron does concern himself with the great problems of existence—human greed, lust, hypocrisy, poverty, inequality, and oppression—and the fundamental import of his satire is positive. *Don Juan* is a true illustration of Matthew Arnold's definition of poetry as a criticism of life. It is Byron's serious criticism of life, and as such it is neither cynical nor shallow, as has often been averred. *Don Juan*, as an epic-satire of all insincerity and all that obstructs human freedom, represents, truly, the flowering of Byron's satiric genius.

BIBLIOGRAPHY

I. WORKS CONSULTED[1]

ANONYMOUS. *Articles and Criticisms on Byron*. (A collection of articles on Byron clipped from various early nineteenth-century periodicals and bound together in a unique set of volumes. The Duke University Library has Volumes 1, 2, and 4–8.)

————. "Juaniana," *The London Magazine* (January 1825), p. 82.

————. "To Christopher North," *Blackwood's Edinburgh Magazine*, XI (April 1822), 465.

BLAQUIERE, EDWARD. *Narrative of a Second Visit to Greece*. London: Printed for George B. Whittaker, 1825.

BLESSINGTON, MARGUERITE, COUNTESS OF. *A Journal of the Conversations of Lord Byron with the Countess of Blessington*. London: Henry Colburn, 1834.

BRANDES, GEORGE. *Main Currents in Nineteenth Century Literature*. London: Heinemann, 1901–5. 6 vols.

BRECKNOCK, ALBERT. *Byron: A Study of the Poet in the Light of New Discoveries*. London: C. Palmer, 1926.

BRISCOE, WALTER ALWYN. *Byron, the Poet*. A Collection of Essays and Addresses . . . . a Centenary Volume. Edited by Walter A. Briscoe. London: G. Routledge and Sons, Ltd., 1924.

BRUCHARD, M. "Notes sur le Don Juanisme." *Mercure de France*, XXVI (1898), 58–73.

BYRON, GEORGE GORDON. *Poetical Works*. London: Humphrey Milford, 1928.

————. *Lord Byron's Correspondence*. Edited by John Murray. London: John Murray, 1922. 2 vols. (See Murray, John.)

---

[1] Part I is a list of works cited as well as of other related works. Part II is a list of the contemporary periodical reviews of *Don Juan* arranged according to canto and alphabetized according to periodical title.

BYRON, GEORGE GORDON. *The Works of Lord Byron: Letters and Journals.* (See Prothero, Rowland E.)

———. *The Works of Lord Byron: Poetry.* (See Coleridge, Ernest Hartley.)

———. *The Ravenna Journal.* Edited with an Introduction by Lord Ernle. London, 1928.

CALVERT, WILLIAM J. *Byron: Romantic Paradox.* Chapel Hill: The University of North Carolina Press, 1935.

CHEW, SAMUEL C. *Byron in England: His Fame and After-Fame.* London: John Murray, 1924.

COLERIDGE, ERNEST HARTLEY. "Byron," *The Encyclopaedia Britannica,* 11th edition, 1910, LV, 897–905.

———. *The Works of Lord Byron: Poetry.* London: John Murray, 1898–1904. 7 vols.

COLLINS, J. CHURTON. *Studies in Poetry and Criticism.* London: George Bell & Sons, 1905.

DALLAS, R. C. *Recollections of the Life of Lord Byron.* Charles Knight, 1824.

DOUGLAS, SIR G. "Don Juan in Literature and Music," *The Cornhill Magazine,* n.s. LI (July 1921), 96–104.

DRINKWATER, JOHN. *The Pilgrim of Eternity: Byron—A Conflict.* New York: Doran, 1925.

EDGCUMBE, RICHARD. *Byron, the Last Phase.* London: John Murray, 1910.

EICHLER, ALBERT. *John Hookham Frere, sein Leben und seine Werke, sein Einfluss auf Lord Byron.* Wien und Leipzig: W. Braumüller, 1905.

ELTON, OLIVER. "The Present Value of Byron," *The Review of English Studies,* I (January 1925), 36.

———. *Survey of English Literature, 1780–1830.* London: Edward Arnold & Company, 1912. 2 vols.

ELZE, KARL. *Lord Byron: A Biography with a Critical Essay on His Place in Literature.* London: John Murray, 1872.

FIELDING, HENRY. *The History of the Adventures of Joseph Andrews.* London: J. M. Dent, 1910.

FUESS, CLAUDE M. *Lord Byron as a Satirist in Verse.* New York: Columbia University Press, 1912.

FUHRMANN, LUDWIG. *Die Belesenheit des Jungen Byron.* Halle: Kinder, 1903.

GALT, JOHN. *Life of Lord Byron.* London: Colburn, 1830.

GENDARME DE BEVOTTE, GEORGES. *La Légende de Don Juan.* Paris: Hachette, 1906.

GORDON, PRYSE LOCKHART. *Personal Memoirs or Reminiscences.* London: Colburn and Bentley, 1830.

GRAHAM, WALTER. *English Literary Periodicals.* New York: Thomas Nelson & Sons, 1930.

GUICCIOLI, COUNTESS TERESA. *My Recollections of Lord Byron.* New York: Harper & Brothers, 1869.

INGPEN, ROGER. *Complete Works of Shelley: Letters* (Julian Editions). London: Ernest Benn, Limited, 1926. 10 vols.

JEAFFRESON, JOHN CORDY. *The Real Lord Byron.* 1883. 2 vols.

KAHN, GUSTAVE. "Don Juan," *Revue Encyclopédique,* VIII (1898), 326–29.

KENNEDY, JAMES. *Conversations on Religion with Lord Byron and Others.* London: John Murray, 1830.

LAMB, LADY CAROLINE. *Glenarvon.* London: Colburn, 1817.

MACAULAY, THOMAS BABINGTON. *Critical and Historical Essays.* New York: Houghton Mifflin, 1900. 3 vols.

MAYNE, ETHEL C. *Byron.* London: Methuen & Company, Ltd., 2d edition, 1924.

——. *The Life and Letters of Anne Isabella, Lady Noel Byron, from Unpublished Papers in the Possession of the late Ralph, Earl of Lovelace;* with an Introduction and Epilogue by Mary, Countess of Lovelace, and twelve illustrations. New York: C. Scribner's Sons, 1929.

MEDWIN, THOMAS. *Journal of the Conversations of Lord Byron, Noted During a Residence with his Lordship at Pisa, in the Years 1821 and 1822.* London: Henry Colburn, 1824.

MOORE, THOMAS. *The Life, Letters, and Journals of Lord Byron.* Complete edition. London, 1908.

MURRAY, JOHN. *Lord Byron's Correspondence Chiefly with Lady Melbourne, Mr. Hobhouse, The Hon. Douglas Kinnaird, and P. B. Shelley.* Edited by John Murray. London: John Murray, 1922. 2 vols.

NICOLSON, HAROLD. *Byron, the Last Journey*. London: Constable, 1924.

PROTHERO, ROWLAND E. *The Works of Lord Byron: Letters and Journals*. London: John Murray, 1898–1902. 6 vols.

QUILLER-COUCH, SIR ARTHUR. *Byron: A Study*. Studies in Literature, Second Series. New York: Putnam's, 1922.

RAYMOND, DORA N. *The Political Career of Lord Byron*. New York: Henry Holt & Company, 1924.

ROSE, WILLIAM STEWART. *The Court and Parliament of Beasts*, freely translated from *The Animali Parlanti* of Giambattista Casti . . . . London: John Murray, 1819.

SCHEVILL, FERDINAND. *A History of Europe from the Reformation to the Present Day*. New York: Harcourt, Brace & Co., 1925.

SHELLEY, PERCY BYSSHE. *Letters of Percy Bysshe Shelley*. Edited by Roger Ingpen. London, 1914.

STEIGER, AUGUST. *Thomas Shadwell's "Libertine."* A Complementary Study to Don Juan—Literature. Berne: Printed by Büchler and Company, 1904.

TICKNOR, GEORGE. *History of Spanish Literature*. Boston: Houghton Mifflin, 1891.

TRELAWNY, EDWARD. *Trelawny's Recollections of the Last Days of Shelley and Byron*. With an Introduction by Edward Dowden. London: Frowde, 1906.

TULLY, RICHARD. *Narrative of a Ten Years' Residence at the Court of Tripoli*. 1816.

WALKER, HUGH. *English Satire and Satirists*. New York: E. P. Dutton, 1925.

WAXMAN, SAMUEL M. "The Don Juan Legend in Literature," *The Journal of American Folk-Lore*, XXI (1908), 184–204.

WHITE, NEWMAN IVEY. *The Unextinguished Hearth*. Durham, N.C.: Duke University Press, 1938.

WISE, THOMAS JAMES. *A Byron Library, A Catalogue of Printed Books, Manuscripts, and Autograph Letters by George Gordon Noel* . . . . London: Printed for private circulation only, 1928.

II. CONTEMPORARY REVIEWS

Cantos I–II

> *Blackwood's Edinburgh Magazine*, V (August 1819), 512–15.
> *The British Critic*, XII (August 1819), 196–204.
> *The Eclectic Review*, XXI (August 1819), 147–56.
> *The Gentleman's Magazine*, LXXXIX (August 1819), 152.
> *The Monthly Review*, LXXXIX (July 1819), 314–21.
> *New Monthly Magazine*, XII (August 1819), 75–78.
> *New Monthly Magazine*, November 1819, p. 381.

Cantos III–V

> *Blackwood's Edinburgh Magazine*, X (August 1821), 107–15.
> *Blackwood's Edinburgh Magazine*, XI (February 1822), 212–13.
> *The British Critic*, XVI (September 1821), 252–55.
> *The Edinburgh Magazine*, LXXXVIII (August 1821), 105–8.
> *The Edinburgh Review*, XXXVI (February 1822), 446–52.
> *The Imperial Magazine*, III (1821), 945–47.
> *The Monthly Review*, XCV (August 1821), 418–20.
> *The Quarterly*, XXVII (July 1822), 476–77.

Cantos VI–VIII

> *Blackwood's Edinburgh Magazine*, XIV (July 1823), 88–92.
> *The British Critic*, XX (August 1823), 178–87.
> *The British Magazine*, August 1, 1823, pp. 273–76.
> *The Edinburgh Magazine*, XCII (August 1823), 190–99.
> *The Gentleman's Magazine*, XCIII (September 1823), 250–52.
> *The Literary Gazette*, July 19, 1823, pp. 451–53.
> *The Portfolio*, I (Numbers xxi and xxii, 1823), 330–48.

Cantos IX–XI

> *Blackwood's Edinburgh Magazine*, XIV (September 1823), 282–93.
> *The British Critic*, XX (September 1823), 524–29.
> *The British Magazine*, September 1, 1823, pp. 296–99.

The Edinburgh Magazine, XCII (September 1823), 357–60.
The Literary Gazette, September 6, 1823, pp. 562–63.

Cantos XII–XIV

The British Critic, XX (December 1823), 662–66.
Knight's Quarterly Magazine, I (December 1823), 343–48.
The Literary Gazette, December 6, 1823, pp. 771–73.

Cantos XV–XVI

The Literary Gazette, April 3, 1824, pp. 212–13.
The Monthly Review, CIII (April 1824), 434.

Index